THE CHRONICLES OF THE CLIFFE
AND SOUTH MALLING
AD 668 - 2003

To Jimmy
with love on our
Anniversary

xxx from
Pauline.

By the same author
The Weathervanes of Sussex
East Sussex Inns
West Sussex Inns
Royal Visitors to Sussex
Night of the Fires – Bonfire in Sussex
The Surrey Quiz Book
Brighton in the Fifties
People and Places of the High Weald

THE CHRONICLES

OF

THE CLIFFE

AND

SOUTH MALLING

AD 668 – 2003

Compiled by

Brigid Chapman

with

line drawings by Helen Fenton

The Book Guild Ltd
Sussex, England

First published in Great Britain in 2003 by
The Book Guild Ltd
25 High Street
Lewes, East Sussex
BN7 2LU

Designed and typeset by
CGB, Lewes

Printed in Great Britain by
Bath Press, Bath

A catalogue record for this book is
available from the British Library

ISBN 1 85776 759 4

CONTENTS

ACKNOWLEDGEMENTS

This book could not have been compiled without the assistance of the people who so kindly took the time to direct me towards recorded facts about the Cliffe and South Malling – particularly John Bleach, Richard Philcox and everyone in the library of the Sussex Archaeological Society; at the East Sussex Records Office; and librarian Alan Hibbs and Tessa Bain at the Lewes branch of East Sussex County Library.

For information about the last half-century I am indebted to Lewes District and Lewes Town Councillor Maureen Messer, Peter Thorpe of the Lewes Rowing Club, Judy Moore of JEM Editorial Services, Lewes, Anne Hilton, secretary of St Michael the Archangel parochial church council and Cliffe churchwarden Mary Chandler.

And above all my deepest thanks to Helen Poole, senior museums officer of the Susssex Archaeological Society, who not only gave me her complete chronology of the church of St Thomas Becket and the Cliffe from 735 to the 1990s, but for her continued interest in and help with the project from start to finish.

PICTURE CREDITS

Permission to use photographs from the collections in their possession has been kindly given to me by the Sussex Archaeological Society, the East Sussex Record Office, the *Sussex Express* and many private collectors. Wherever possible pictures are individually credited. Those that are not are 'owner unknown' – or taken by the compiler.

INTRODUCTION

The information in these *Chronicles* is, wherever possible, from original documents and records and from contemporary accounts in newspapers, beginning in 1752 with the *Sussex Weekly Advertiser*. Another invaluable source of information about the Cliffe and South Malling has been the *Spicilegia sive Collectanea ad Historian et Antiguatatis Municipii Vicinioe Lewensis, 1812-1820,* an unpublished manuscript by Thomas Woollgar, presented to the Sussex Archaeological Society by Sir Henry Wagner.

There are few published details about this man to whom historians with an interest in this locality owe so much. The Reverend T W Horsfield, paying tribute to him in his *History and Antiquities of Lewes,* says that Woollgar was born in Deal, Kent in 1761 and his parents moved to Lewes two years after the birth of their son. The boy went to Lewes Grammar School and then 'immediately entered upon commercial pursuits, in which the early part of his life was chiefly engaged'.

What these commercial pursuits were Horsfield does not disclose. Neither does the *Gentlemen's Magazine* in the obituary it published after Thomas Woollgar's death in 1821. Young Thomas was, in fact, a draper's assistant who in 1794, the year he married Anne, daughter of John Webb, became a partner in the Lewes firm of 'Weller and Woolger, Drapers', which is listed in the Universal British Directory of 1793. 'During the intervals of business he studied medicine and natural history; to the former science he became so much attached that he would have adopted it as a profession, had circumstances been favourable,' continues Horsfield. 'Four years after this, he retired altogether from an occupation which daily became less congenial to his habits, intending to devote himself to literary and scientific researches.'

Woollgar published little – just a few articles in the *Gentlemen's Magazine* and some contributions to *English Botany*. What he did do, with painstaking diligence and in a very fair hand, earning the eternal gratitude of the compiler of these *Chronicles,* was to transcribe, in volume II of his *Spicilegia,* the manorial and parochial details of the Cliffe and South Malling. He included 'A Description of the Parish of Saint Thomas in the Cliff near Lewes (Copied from an Ms)', a copy of the report of the committee appointed to produce a scheme for the widening of Cliffe High Street in 1827, an account of the 'Deanery of Malling and Southmalling in Sussex', and details of the 'Cliff Cemetery or the Burying Ground'.

Three years after the death of his wife in 1815 Thomas Woollgar suffered from an abscess on the liver. He recovered, but remained an invalid until his death on 22 December 1821. He was buried in the Webb family vault at St John the Baptist church, Southover, and there is a memorial tablet to him and his wife in All Saints' church. It was erected by his son, John Webb Woollgar, who like his father had other than business interests. He was a Fellow of the Royal Astronomical Society as well as being a solicitor, in partnership with J T Aukland. The firm of Woollgar and Aukland, in 'High Street, Cliff', is listed in *Robson's Directory* for 1839 as clerks to the Cliff Commissioners.

BRIGID CHAPMAN
SPRING 2003

1. FROM THE IRON AGE TO THE DISSOLUTION

BC-1600

Between the steep chalk slopes of Malling Hill, the Coombe, Cliffe Hill and the eastern banks of the River Ouse is the Cliffe. When Iron Age farmers were ploughing the terraced fields on Malling Hill, setting up their earthworks on Mount Caburn and drying their corn in ovens at Ranscombe, the land between the hills on either side of the Ouse river was covered with water. Further to the south, where the Glynde Reach now joins the main river, there was virtually an inland sea. By AD 410, when the Roman legions were withdrawn from Britain to deal with troubles at home, the sea had retreated and exposed the levels on which the Cliffe and part of South Malling stand.

Coins of Domitian, son of Vespasian, and of Antonius Pius who succeeded Hadrian of wall fame in AD 138, have been found not all that far beneath the surface on the Levels and there are a number of other indications of a Roman presence in the area.

In the 1950s, when the Church Lane housing estate at South Malling was being built, a 50-metre metalled section of an ancient road was uncovered and beside it a group of seven Romano-British cremation burials. Two Saxon skeletons were also found there, one on the metalling of the road itself, together with an iron knife, a belt ring and a bronze saucer-shaped brooch.

The first settlement on the flood plain of which there is any written record is the monastery at Malling. It is believed to have been founded about a century after Pope Gregory had sent Augustine to Britain with, so say *The Anglo-Saxon Chronicles*, 'a good many monks who preached the gospel to the English people'.

The only reliable information about this monastery before the Conquest is from a thirteenth-century copy of its foundation charter. The original, dated *c*765 was, said John Leland, an antiquarian writing in the sixteenth century, destroyed in a fire.

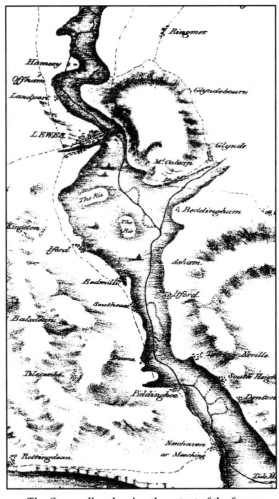

The Ouse valley showing the extent of the former inland sea and the river, with its pre-1795 meanders indicated by double dotted lines.

The charter poses as many questions as it answers. To begin with it states:

I, Aldwulf the King, having been asked by my thegn Hunlaf that I would deign to grant him a small estate wherein to build a minster, agreeing to his prayers do for the benefit of my soul for ever freely make over and grant that estate to which he appears to refer . . .

It goes on to set out the boundaries of the various areas of woodland, pasture and pig pannage in Lindfield, Stanmer and Burleigh that form the 'small estate', bounded on the west by the Roman road from London to Portslade and on the east by the Ouse. It then

The Grimm engraving of the ruins at Old Malling as they were in the late eighteenth century.

muddies the waters by concluding:

I, Aldwulf the King have in unfeigned assent with my own hand signed this grant for the building of a monastery, and the increase of those there serving God and St Michael, although they were founded long since by the pious men of former times.

Who were these pious men? Leland, in his *Collectanea,* names one of them – Caedwalla, king of the West Saxons, who in AD 688 was converted to Christianity and went to Rome to be baptised by Pope Sergius I. He died seven days later, still in his baptismal robes. The Leland entry states:

Collegium de Southmalling. Habet Decanum. Vix uno a Lewes milliari distat. Cedwalla rex primis fundator. Chartae I. Donat combustae.

Where Leland's 'college of priests about a thousand paces from Lewes, founded by Caedwalla, the first charter of which was destroyed by fire' was originally built is as much a matter of conjecture as who built it.

The Reverend Edward Turner, writing in the *Sussex Archaeological Collections* of 1852, places the monastery 'rather more than half a mile to the north of the town of Lewes, on a verdant eminence, gently rising above the banks of the River Ouse'.

This site – occupied since the sixteenth century by Old Malling Farmhouse – and the South Malling site of the college at the time of the Dissolution, are both on the line of a Roman road and both once had river crossings. Henry's knights used the ford at South Malling to flee from de Montfort's troops after the Battle of Lewes and a survey of the river bed has revealed the piles and planks of a causeway stretching from Old Malling to Landport.

On the list of those for whose souls the secular canons of St Michael the Archangel were required daily to pray was:

The Venerable Father Theobald, Archbishop of Canterbury, who built and endowed the church of the said college.

It seems reasonable to suppose that the original Saxon timber building at Old Malling was so badly damaged by the fire in which its charter was destroyed that it had to be rebuilt. This was done, presumably by Theobald in the mid-twelfth century, but whether on the same site, which the remains still to be seen there suggest, or at South Malling, is a matter of debate.

Perhaps the secular canons, who succeeded the Benedictines at Caedwalla's monastery some time before the Domesday survey of 1086, made use of both sites before finally basing their operations exclusively at South Malling.

The restored remains at Old Malling

The great storm of 16 October 1987 brought a branch of a tree crashing down on to the wall depicted in the Grimm engraving (see facing page). Hugh Court, the then owner of the sixteenth-century half of Old Malling Farmhouse which was divided into two in the 1970s, tried to interest English Heritage and a number of archaeological groups in taking an active part in restoring the section damaged by the tree and conserving what was left on the possible site of one of the earliest religious houses in the county. However, in the end the new owners, Tony and Sue Redshaw, did it themselves.

'Luckily we were helped by the insurers,' said Sue. 'It seemed that the Grade II listed wall in the garden was classed as a party wall and therefore covered for storm damage'.

They did much more. They incorporated into the design of their garden some of the large standing stones they found scattered around the area and also used a quantity of excavated material to build part of what Sue describes as 'a pseudo ruin'. Before the restoration work was started the exact position of every stone of the structure in the garden, as well as all the standing stones in its

Tidying up after the 1987 hurricane brought a tree crashing down onto the ruins. Photo: Sussex Express

vicinity, were recorded. Members of the Lewes Archaeological Group spent every Sunday afternoon of the cold and wet winter of 1987-88 marking each one on to a scale plan. They discovered a dovecote in front of the ten foot bank at the southern end of the medieval wall. Some of its nesting boxes had been blocked off with lime mortar, as had the

The scene today. St Francis, bought in Italy – there were no Benedictines available – stands before the wall, with the 'pseudo ruin' to the left.

11

inside of a bricked-up window. Many of the chalk blocks used in its construction were of odd sizes and there was the arch of a late medieval drain at the base of the building.

The presence of the dovecote poses the question – is it the 'Dovehouse of the Deanery' mentioned in Thomas Cranmer's petition to the Court of Augmentation for the return to his archbishopric of the manor lands that had been given to it by Baldred in AD 830? If so, it confirms Old Malling as the original site of the Benedictine monastery founded by Aldwulf.

Cranmer's claim details the acreage of each parcel of land and its location in relation to the 'mansion of the archbishop'. It includes:

> . . . two crofts of land now called Dovehouse croft and sometime was two crofts divided and lieth to the Dovehouse of the Deanery and containeth three acres, one messuage or cottage called Ballards lying nigh the said Dovehouse croft and lying on the south side of the way that leadeth to the church at Malling.

A possible scenario, accepting that Malling House occupies the site of the mansion, is that the dovehouse of the deanery – taking 'deanery' in its administrative rather than structural sense – was built on the original Old Malling site with materials recovered from the building damaged by the fire in which the charter was destroyed.

The sixteenth-century part of Old Malling Farmhouse itself appears to have been built within the foundations of a considerably older building. The wall between the living room and the kitchen is 4ft thick and in it is set a window on to the stairs, the surround of which has now been incorporated into the restored southern wall of the former dovecote. In a corner of the living room ceiling there is an Early English carved stone corbel.

A map prepared in 1620 shows three buildings at 'Old Mawling', the smaller of which could be the dovecote. At 'South Mawling' it shows just one large building, presumably the 'suitable manse near the churchyard' that Archbishop Warham had built at his own expense in 1515 to provide accommodation for the sacrist and the vicars who accompanied the canons when they were in residence. The canons, who were required by statute to spend forty days a year at the college, had their own houses and gardens but the vicars they brought with them had to stay with anyone in the locality who would give them bed and board. Having his priests sleeping around in this fashion disturbed the archbishop. He considered it:

> offensive to God, and the church generally, and especially to the Collegiate Church of South Malling.

The 'suitable manse' became the 'capital mansion' of Malling Deanery which was bought from John Evelyn by William Kempe in 1632 and rebuilt in the 1750s by his great grandson, Sergeant-at-Law William Kempe. Since then it has been much altered and today only the carvings on the arched surround of a doorway in the North Wing remain as evidence of its Tudor origins.

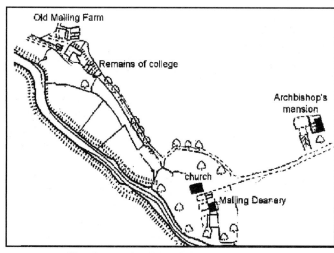

Sketch map showing relative positions of the college buildings.

12

Earliest inhabitants are buried on the hill

*c*2000 BC

The burnt bones of a child who lived and died on Cliffe Hill in the early Bronze Age are now in the British Museum. He or she – the bones are too charred for the sex to be determined – was buried in the long barrow on the hill crest immediately above the Coombe and known locally as the Camel's Humps. The name describes the shape the barrow acquired when someone cut a trench through the middle of it and banked the earth up into mounds on either side. A possible culprit was Lewes palaeontologist Gideon Mantell, for he notes in his *Journal* on 27 January 1821:

> Accompanied Mr Durrant on the Hill and had a tumulus opened. It contained a skeleton . . .

The 50ft diameter barrow above the chalk quarry in South Street was opened in 1930 and found to contain teeth and broken and burnt bones of a number of adults and an eight-year-old child as well as some pieces of pottery, a number of worked flints and

shells, and fragments of two cinerary urns. One of the urns, when restored, was found to be 6ins in height and the other was twice as tall.

A well-defined grave was found the following year 8ft below the chalk. It was 2ft 6ins in length and it contained a milk tooth and the bones of a five-year-old child.

This barrow seems to have served as a cemetery from the Middle Bronze Age to the La Téne period (*c*1500BC-AD 100). It was visited by the Romans, who dropped fifteen coins from the reign of Gallienus (AD 260-8) on the site and five from the fourth century when Constantine was emperor. Visiting Victorians were not so careless with their cash, leaving behind only a threepenny bit, dated 1861, and a brass thimble with the inscription 'Live and let live'.

DOMESDAY HOUSE COUNT

1086

The Domesday survey, after listing under the heading LAND OF WILLIAM OF WARENNE (Lewes Rape) the tributes and tolls of the Borough of Lewes, states: 'In the Rape of Pevensey 39 inhabited dwellings and 20 uninhabited'.

The commissioners who conducted the survey retained the Anglo Saxon division of the county into hundreds and hides and added to them an administrative top tier called a rape. Sussex is the only county in England to be so divided.

Were these fifty Pevensey Rape houses, mentioned in virtually the same breath as the Borough of Lewes, in the Cliffe? It seems reasonable to suppose that they were as the river Ouse forms the boundary between the two rapes.

MANOR FARM

1093

The Archbishop's manor of Malling was originally a single unit held by Godfrey of Malling 'to farm for £90'. When it was split up among a number of tenants Godfrey kept a holding for which he paid fifty shillings a year.

Becket murder 'miracle' at Malling

30 December 1170

Archbishop Thomas Becket, a benefactor and a frequent visitor to the Collegiate Church of St Michael the Archangel at Malling, was slain by four knights in his own cathedral yesterday. Today

The table of Sussex marble, mounted on a modern stand of the same material, is in Anne of Cleves House museum in Lewes.

the four, named as Reginald Fitz-Urse, William de Tracy, Richard le Breton and Hugh de Moreville, arrived at the Archbishop's mansion at South Malling for a night's rest on their flight to France. They were sitting by the fire in the great hall when the 'miracle' occurred. The table on which they had placed their blood-stained gauntlets and swords began to shake violently and their weapons were thrown to the floor. This occurred twice 'though the table was large and massive and firmly fixed and no sign of movement could be seen when lights were brought' says Dean Stanley, who records the 'miracle' in his *Memorials of Canterbury Cathedral.*

CHICKEN AND EGG COUNT

1285

Hens and eggs were units of currency for tenants who had common rights within the forests in the Sussex manors of the Archbishops of Canterbury. Owing for this year, according to the account rolls in the Canterbury Custumal, is a total of 148 hens and 490 eggs.

FERRY FEE

The same rolls show that Chune (or June) at Bote was on to a good thing. She leased a croft on the banks of the Ouse at Malling for 10d a year and charged 6d a time to ferry people across the river in her boat.

Knights and their horses drown in the mud

LEWES 14 MAY 1264:

After the battle that had raged in and around Lewes all day Simon de Montfort's men kept up their pursuit of King Henry's defeated forces. As night fell, the western approach to Cliffe bridge was jammed with the pursued and their pursuers.

In an attempt to avoid the chaos at the bridge, and the fear that the unfenced wooden structure would not bear the weight of men on horseback and in armour, some knights used the ford beside the bridge to cross the river and others made their way to the fords at Southerham and Landport. Some, in panic, tried to splash their way through the marshes.

The *Lanercost Chronicle* reports that many attempting to ford the river sank into the mud and were drowned or suffocated. The bodies of a number of knights, still sitting on their horses in full armour and with swords in their hands, were recovered from the river bed several days after the battle.

NOTE: The first reference to a bridge over the Ouse at Lewes is in the Pipe Rolls, those national accounts which give details, county by county, of revenue raised locally for specific purposes. In 1159-60 the sum of 65s for the repair of Lewes bridge is recorded.

Victim? Murderer? Eye witness? Who did build Cliffe church?

*c*1170

CLIFFE church, originally a chapel of ease of the college at Malling, was built, so it is said, by direct order of Archbishop Thomas Becket, to whose martyrdom it is dedicated. It is also suggested that its building was financed by one of the murderers as a penance for committing an act of sacrilege or by someone who witnessed the dastardly act but did nothing to stop it.

Becket, like Theobald before him, looked favourably upon the canons at Malling. He confirmed his predecessor's grants to the college, and added a gift of his own:

> . . . to the church of St Michael at Mallyng and the free Canons therein, the manse and demesne lands belonging thereto.

The Fraternity of St Thomas in the Cliffe, a cell of the college at South Malling, which owned a large tract of land in the parish, is linked with Thomas Becket not only by name. When some old buildings opposite the church, formerly occupied by the Fraternity, were being pulled down in the nineteenth century the arms of Archbishop Becket were found carved upon the chimney breast of one of them.

Thomas Woollgar, in his *Description of the Parish of St Thomas in the Cliff, near Lewes,* sug-

gests that it is more likely that the builder of the church was Hugh de Boscham, a personal assistant to the archbishop and present in the cathedral at his murder – during which he kept in the background in case he suffered the same fate as his master.

De Boscham wrote a number of books about Becket 'and may, not without reason, be presumed to have built and consecrated the church to his master's memory', says Woollgar.

The list of vicars is inscribed on a board in the church tower. It begins in 1320 with John de Arundel, a monk from Bayham Abbey, who remained there until 1349.

In the fifteenth century the status of the living was changed and the vicars, who did not receive all the tithes paid by the parishioners for the upkeep of the church, became rectors, who did.

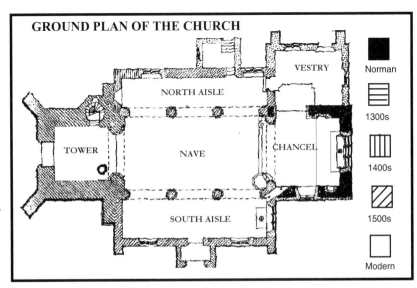

GROUND PLAN OF THE CHURCH

VESTRY

NORTH AISLE

TOWER
NAVE
CHANCEL

SOUTH AISLE

Norman

1300s

1400s

1500s

Modern

<table>
<tr><td>

TAKING THE MEASURE OF A MEDIEVAL MANOR

</td><td>

Medieval measures varied from manor to manor. A hide, which consisted of four virgates or yardlands, could consist of 60 acres or less in Sussex. At the Archbishop's manor of Southerham the virgate (Latin – *virgata terra*) contained about 12 acres of land, giving a hide a total of some 48 acres. The length of the rod, pole or perch that was used to mark out land that had to be ploughed in strips governed the exact acreage of the virgate. At South Malling these rods were 'by ancient custom' 16ft in length.

</td></tr>
</table>

PARISHES SHARE A CEMETERY

1283

The first indication of the difficulties the parishes of Cliffe and South Malling were to have with their burial grounds occurred this year. As access to the graveyard at South Malling was not possible in the bad weather Archbishop John Peckham agreed to licence the parishes' use of the cemetery at Ringmer.

MARKET GRANT

14 October 1331

Cliffe's market charter of 1409 was anticipated by a grant of special grace to the Archbishops of Canterbury for a weekly market on Thursdays and an annual fair before, on and after 29 December – the feast of St Thomas the Martyr to whom the parish church is dedicated.

When Southerham had a chapel and a convent

*c*1200

Southerham was a farming community of sufficient size to have its own chapel in the thirteenth century. It was dedicated to St Mary Magdalen and there is mention of it in the *Great Taxation of Pope Nicholas* in 1291 which put a valuation of £6,948 19s 9½d on all the benefices in Sussex. It also had a convent which the *Victoria County History* describes as:

> A house of Benedictine nuns founded by Richard, Archbishop of Canterbury 1174-1183, mentioned by Gervase the Chronicler *c*1200 as one of the religious houses of Sussex. Suppressed by Archbishop Hubert 1193-1205 who granted its lands and buildings to Guy the Prior and the Canons of St Gregory, Canterbury. It was refounded by Archbishop Boniface 1241-1270.

There are no further references to a convent at Southerham. It was obviously refounded elsewhere.

The chapel had become derelict by 1545 when the possessions of the college at South Malling were surrendered to the Crown. It was turned into a dwelling and five years later manorial records show that Edward Brown was paying an annual rental of fourpence for 'the messuage sometime the chapel of Sothram'.

James Lambert senior painted several versions of the chapel site in 1780 as part of his commission from antiquarian Sir William Burrell for a series of Sussex landscapes. Some of them show, to the right of a thatched cottage surrounded by trees, what could well be the crumbling walls of the derelict chapel. In 1800, together with other property in Southerham, this cottage became part of the estate of the Gages of Firle. It was finally demolished in 1836-37.

The three sisters and their sheep

1305

The climate changes that resulted in almost constant flooding in the Ouse Valley in the later years of the fourteenth century caused land prices to fall to a pathetic 2d an acre and for 400 acres of the Archbishop's land at Southerham to be converted into a permanent fishery known as the Brodewater.

However, before these successive years of wet weather and problems with the silting up of the sea outlet at Seaford put paid to farming on the flood plain, a well-ordered system of food production was in operation in the Archbishop's manor. Tenants held their land in return for some stipulated service, or for cash, or for a combination of the two. Those on service tenancies had four weeks holiday a year, two at Christmas and one each at Easter and Whitsun, and the *Custumals of the Archbishop of Canterbury's Manors in Sussex* make it clear that:

If anyone should be ill he shall be quit of work for two weeks.

Women as well as men were accepted as customary tenants. A 1305 rental shows that at Southerham Juliana at Dene and her sisters, Agnes and Lettice, had a 24-acre sheep walk and 1½ acres of meadow and 3 acres of pasture for eight beasts for which they paid £1 a year – ten shillings at Midsummer and ten shillings at Michaelmas. They were also allowed to keep 120 ewes 'on the lord's pasture if the lord will' and had to give 'a halfpenny every Saturday from Lady Day to Michaelmas for butter.' The Archbishop was, however, to have all the wool of the aforesaid sheep.

The service side of their contract required the sisters to 'plough one acre for oats and sow and hoe another and reap the corn growing thereon and make it ready for carting'.

ARE CANONS IN ARREARS OF RENT?

1331

Five houses and six plots of land in the Cliffe, leased by Joan, 'widow of the smith', for twenty pence a year, were sold by her heirs to the Canons of South Malling. 'It is not known for certain if the aforesaid 20d is paid with the 4s rent which the aforesaid Canons have paid to the Archbishop' states the Custumal. 'And if it is not they are eight years and more in arrears . . . but Stephen the clerk will inform us on these matters.'

WATER BOARD

1422

A Commission of Sewers has been set up to rebuild the river banks and improve the drainage system of the Ouse Valley from the port of Seaford to Fletching. Among the nine landowners named as Commissioners was Thomas Nelond, Prior of Lewes.

JUSTICE'S STEWARD ACCUSED OF RIGGING THE JURY
1377

John Harold, steward to county justice, Sir William de Echingham, has moved the 25 miles from the village that bears his master's name to a house in the Cliffe where he entertains Sir William when he has business in Lewes. Just how honest a steward John was is in doubt. Court records show that he may have been involved – with his sons and two others – in some jury rigging in an assize case concerning the ownership of the freehold of a tenement at Malling. He was also behind with the rent of a meadow and sheep pen at Ringmer.

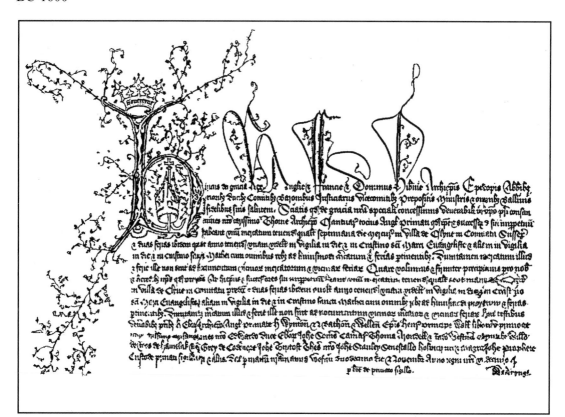

A facsimile of the market charter is in Cliffe church. The original is in the East Sussex Record Office.

KING HENRY'S MIRACLE CURE

22 July 1498

A multitude of miracles have been attributed to King Henry VI, mainly for political reasons.

Miracle No 157, on a list just published, took place 'at Cliffe near the monastery of Lewes'. Joan Reynolds, who had died of the plague and had been sewn up in her shroud was, it is claimed, restored to life through her mother's prayers to the king.

❖ ❖ ❖

King signs Cliffe's market charter

12 November 1409

At Westminster today the king granted the Archbishop of Canterbury and his successors the right for ever to hold a market in the Cliffe every Wednesday and two fairs there every year. Dates fixed for the three-day fairs are before, on and after St Mark's Day (6 May) and before, on and the day after the feast of St Matthew (22 October). The May fair is for black cattle and the October one for sheep. As the charter states, these dates were chosen in order not to conflict with neighbouring fairs. It starts:

> Henry, by the grace of God, King of England and France, and Lord of Ireland: To the Archbishops, Bishops, Abbots, Priors, Dukes, Earls, Barons, Justices, Sheriffs, and to all their faithful officers and bailiffs greeting: Know ye, that by our special grace, we have granted to the most reverend father in Christ, our most dear cousin, Thomas, Archbishop of Canterbury, Primate of All England, that he and his successors do for ever hold one Market, to be held every week on Wednesday, in the town of the Cliffe in the County of Sussex, and two Fairs to be held there every year (that is to say) one on the eve of St Mark the Evangelist . . . with all such things belonging to such markets and fairs, so that the said market and the said fairs be not to the hurt of neighbouring markets and fairs . . .

Saxon manor grant makes parishes 'peculiars'

1443

THE Archbishop of Canterbury's peculiar jurisdiction over a number of parishes in the diocese of Chichester is a result of Baldred's grant to the see of Canterbury in AD 830 of the Manor of Malling – a twenty-eight mile wide swathe of land stretching from Lewes to the Kent border and containing, according to the Domesday survey, 219 villagers, thirty-five smallholders, forty-three crofts, five mills, an estimated 2,000 eels and 355 pigs.

In the absence of the archbishop, his power over the parishes in the manor devolved upon the dean of the Collegiate Church of St Michael's at Malling. It was the dean, according to the statutes signed by Archbishop Stafford in 1443, who had to visit all the churches within the Malling deanery once a year, punish any irregularities of priest or parishioners, see that all fees were paid, defaulters dealt with and arrange for any necessary repairs.

As well as the archbishop's 'peculiars' of Buxted and its chapel at Uckfield; Malling with its chapels at the Cliffe and Southerham; Lewes, Edburton, Framfield, Glynde, Isfield, Mayfield, Ringmer, Stanmer and Wadhurst; the Malling deanery was responsible for the churches at Lindfield and Tarring and for the chapel at Patching in West Sussex.

In the thirteenth century Richard, rector of Tarring, rebelled against Malling deanery having control over his church and its chapels but Canterbury ruled against him. He was told that the dean of Malling was the final authority in any disputes within Tarring parish and he and his chaplains must attend the rural chapters at Malling whenever they were required to do so.

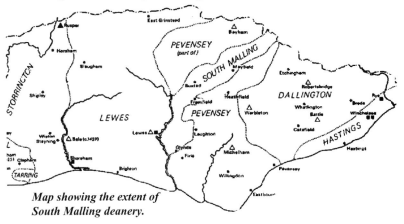

Map showing the extent of South Malling deanery.

CHURCH IN DANGER OF COLLAPSE
1440

A survey has shown that the college's own church at Malling is in such a dilapidated state that it is likely to collapse at any moment. Archbishop Stratford, on discovering that no money had been put aside for repairs, has directed the dean and canons each to pay 6s 8d on 8 October every year into a repair fund. The cash collected is to be placed in a chest with two locks and keys and kept in the college treasury.

CADE REBELS PARDONED
July 1450

Twelve men of the Cliffe who took part in Jack Cade's rebellion, appear as named individuals in the general pardon given for 'gathering together against the statutes of the realm to the contempt of the King's estate'. The twelve include merchant John Wryther; yeomen John Lardener, John Chamberlain, Thomas Podey, John Worthe and William Holybon; together with two chapmen, a glover, a smith and a sheep shearer.

Dean Robert's dissolution deals

1544

WHEN Henry VIII removed England from the authority of Rome and declared himself Head of the Church the resultant changes sent a social shock wave throughout the kingdom. The suppression of 616 religious houses threw thousands out of work as labour intensive arable land was turned into more commercially viable pasture. The process of the dissolution was, however, carried out in a business-like and civilised fashion at South Malling.

Before the college was finally surrendered to the king, commissioners were appointed to agree what pensions and annuities the canons should receive and what portion of 'the goodes of the said College' should be retained by them. The financial arrangements seem to have been concluded satisfactorily for on 10 March 1545 the deed of surrender was signed and sealed by the dean, Robert Peterson, and four members of the college.

Malling was not the first religious house that Dean Robert had surrendered. On 16 November 1537 he handed over Lewes Priory, signing the deed 'Robert Croham', the name he assumed when he became Prior of Lewes in 1526. He took over at a time when this Cluniac foundation was in a state of moral and spiritual decline. If Dr Richard Layton's report to Thomas Cromwell is to be believed, it was a hotbed of 'corruption of both sorts, avowterers (fornicators) and sodomites. And what is worse, treason'.

Prior Robert, when these failings were brought to his attention in October 1535, is said to have fallen to his knees and begged for mercy.

However, he was soon on his feet again and negotiating for the best deal he could get. He sold the priory's stock of salt fish to Thomas Cromwell's nephew for £48 17s 4d; arranged for his younger brother, Peter, to take over the farm at Swanborough and proposed that he, Robert, should also live there 'because I have been brought up in these parts'.

The white wax seal of the college.

He was appointed treasurer of Chichester cathedral in 1539 and a few months later he took charge of the South Malling Deanery, having persuaded Dean Nicholas Heth to resign, after barely two years in office, by offering him a pension of £15 a year for the rest of his life.

Dean Robert did well out of the surrender of the college at South Malling. He received an annuity of £100 in compensation for loss of office and was inducted to the rectory of Shere in Surrey.

It seems that he had little difficulty in accepting the rules and ritual of the reformed church for he was still Rector of Shere and Chancellor of Chichester when he died in 1555. He left detailed instructions in his will for his obsequies and the disposal of his not inconsiderable fortune. Richard Brysley, Archdeacon of Lewes, was his executor but refused to act and the estate was administered by another of Dean Robert's brothers, William Peterson.

Crown sells the college

1546

THE deanery and college of South Malling and the estates that went with it were sold by the Crown to Sir Thomas Palmer two years after their surrender. Thomas was the youngest of the three 'medically miraculous' sons of Sir Edward Palmer of Angmering. The boys were said to have been born on three successive Sundays – the first on Whit Sunday, the second on Trinity Sunday and Thomas, the youngest, the Sunday after. All three were soldiers of great courage and were knighted for valour by Henry VIII.

For an investment of one thousand marks, about £330, 'Sir Thomas Palmer, the Younger Knight' acquired 'the scite of the College of South Malling with the demesne lands of the same, together with all the manors, landes, rectories, tenements . . .' It would give him an income, after tax, of £110 0s 8¼d a year but he did not profit from it for long.

Palmer literally lost his head by picking the wrong side in the conflict over who was to succeed the young king, Edward VI, who was dying of consumption. He made the mistake of siding with John Dudley, the Duke of Northumberland, whose daughter-in-law, Lady Jane Grey, was proclaimed queen on 7 July 1553. Ten days later she was a prisoner in the Tower and Northumberland and his supporters, Sir Thomas Palmer among them, were beheaded on Tower Hill.

Archbishop reclaims his mansion

1553

Thomas Cranmer has successfully petitioned the Crown for the return of the 'mansion house of the archbishop' and some forty acres of land surrounding it which, he claimed, belonged by right of inheritance and of possession to the archbishopric of Canterbury.

The Court of Augmentations and Revenues agreed with him. It ruled that the dean and canons of the collegiate church of St Michael had, at the time of the dissolution, been tenants at will of the lands belonging to the archbishopric and these should be returned, together with whatever rents the Crown had received from them, to the archbishop as lord of the manor of Malling. With a few exceptions the lands in the schedule are described as 'lying nigh to the mansion of the archbishop' – the site of which is occupied today by Malling House.

STATE CLAIMS CASH OWED TO A SUICIDE

2 May 1553

Thomas Whitfield jumped into a well at his house in the Cliffe and 'feloniously killed himself'. That was the verdict of an inquest jury when it considered the case.

Twelve years later a bond was produced to the King's Bench showing that on the day of his death Whitfield was owed £30 by Robert Pennell, who had predeceased him by six months.

Because Whitfield committed suicide, the debt incurred by Pennell was payable to the Crown and action was taken against his son, Peter Pennell, for its recovery. Peter contested the claim but had to pay up.

BRIDGE MUST BE REBUILT

26 March 1563

As a result of a number of complaints about the ruinous state of Cliffe bridge an order was made at the Quarter Sessions in Lewes today for it to be rebuilt.

The cost of the work, estimated at £87 5s 3d, is to be shared equally between the Rapes of Lewes and Pevensey.

BELL, COPE AND CANDLESTICKS

1 March 1554

When the church at Malling was dismantled one of its six bells was given to Cliffe church and the rest sold for £44. The weight of the bell delivered to Mr Everard and Mr Brown was 7cwt 2qrs 17lbs.

St Thomas's church was also given a pair of altar candlesticks, a chalice, a green velvet cope, three silk curtains, an altar cloth, the ceiling of the Lady Chapel, the seats of the church at Malling, the stone of its walls and the case of a pair of organs.

POLE POSITION

5 March 1579

John Savage fell into the Ouse at South Malling and was drowned when the quant pole he was using stuck between two stakes on the bank. In trying to free it he was thrown out of his boat into the water.

WAY OUT

8 November 1557

An inquest jury recorded that Joan Bray, who lived in the Cliffe, bought a halfpenny-worth of ratsbane and 'mixed it with a draught and drank it, thereby murdering herself.'

Memorial brasses stolen from tombs

19 November 1553

A survey ordered by the Queen's Remembrancer reports in detail on the structure of the collegiate church at Malling – and the taking ways of the local inhabitants. It reveals that twenty-nine brasses with images and writings upon them were 'beaten out and stolen' from marble tombstones set in the floor of the nave and chancel. Horsham stone that had fallen from the chancel roof because the rafters had rotted had been 'taken and embezzled'. The steeple had been stripped of its lead by a bullock herdsman claiming to be a surveyor. He had given away two to three hundredweight and left the rest lying in rows on the roof. Horses, cattle and pigs had 'come daily to the church, in summer for shade and in the winter for shelter' and had badly damaged the floor from which many of the decorative Flanders tiles had been stolen.

From the survey, which was carried out by 'neighbours and men of most skill and experience' – Edward Gage, William Newton, and William Evered, advised by bellfounder William Wynberry and two masons and a carpenter – it is possible to get some idea of the appearance of the church, the body of which was covered with shingle 'so long unrepaired that it is wholly decayed and rotten with great holes clearly uncovered so it rains in'.

Its walls were of flint and roughcast, covered with mortar on the outside and faced with chalk blocks on the inside. The pillars, buttresses and steeple, 'in many places and for the most part', were of sandstone. The tower, which housed six bells, is described as 'flat roofed and embattled and wholly covered with lead'. The chancel roof was covered half with lead and half with Horsham stone and the floor of the nave and chancel was paved with Flanders tiles.

CHURCH HOLDS A CLEARANCE SALE

Local landowners did well out of the St Michael's church clearance sale. 'Mr Gage of Firle' had forty loads of Horsham stone at 5s 4d a load and 3cwt of lead for 24s; Mr Chatfield paid 2d for 'a planke'; and Thomas Mylton bought the chancel roof and body of the church for £7 10s. The font went to John Stempe for 20d. Mr Morley had a wheel and an old clock for 10d, a window for 2s and the glass of a window for 6d. The total amount realised was £37 9s 2d.

2. CLIFFE IS IN BUSINESS BY ROAD AND RIVER

1601-1700

The boom in business that started in the days of Elizabeth continued throughout the seventeenth century, regardless of gunpowder plots, the killing of a king, a civil war, and yet more religious unrest. The Cliffe was well placed for commerce, built as it was in the form of a cross on the eastern bank of the Ouse. The streets are aligned to the four cardinal points, and named after them. Travellers coming along North Street (now Malling Street), East Street (Chapel Hill) and South Street were funnelled along West Street at the end of which a wooden bridge arched across the Ouse. The river, more often than the roads, was used for the movement of goods and many merchants in the Cliffe and Malling carried on a lively import and export trade through the port of Newhaven.

The butcher, the baker, the candlemaker were all in West Street, along with draper Thomas Moseley, hatter Thomas Robinson, brewer Robert Rosan, builder Robert Lancaster, goldsmith James Emery, dyer John Homard and others whose names were not a matter of record for their religious beliefs. For when not earning money the tradesmen of the Cliffe appeared to devote their time either to attending meetings of Dissenters or informing against, and physically attacking, those who did attend such meetings.

They certainly paid little attention to public health. Nothing was done to improve the drainage system as more and more houses were crammed into the low lying main street of the Cliffe. The result, according to Paul Dunvan, whose *Lee's History of Lewes* was published in 1735, was that:

... fevers of the most malignant kind have frequently broken out in the Cliffe ... The augmentation of the poor rates on account of such sickness, has in the course of five years, cost the parish more than it would to deepen the sewers, so far as to procure a constant current of fresh water through each ... The porous soil of the more western part of this parish, being constantly saturated with the stagnant sullage or filth of the vicinity, their well and pump water is thereby impregnated with noisome and disgusting particles.

How many houses there were in the Cliffe and how few at Malling can be seen on this sketch of a map prepared in 1620 by George Randoll. West Street is drawn in sufficient detail to show the House of Correction and the market house by the church.

RECTOR WITH A REPUTATION

1611–1643

Anthony Huggett led a colourful religious and personal life in the thirty-one years he was rector of Cliffe church.

He was removed from both Cliffe and Glynde for his 'severity to parishioners for going to other church-es' and for refusing the sacrament to a lame man who could not kneel to receive it. In 1616 he was involved in a case of defamation against Thomas Taylor and was bound over at Quarter Sessions for a number of misdemeanours.

Huggett was included among eight Sussex clergymen who featured in Colonel John White's *Century of Scandalous Malignant Priests* which the House of Commons ordered to be printed in 1634. According to the colonel the rector of Cliffe church led a grossly immoral life. He treated his wife with great cruelty and caused the death of his unborn child by kicking its mother in the stomach so causing her to miscarry. All this from a parson who, in 1615, published a sermon entitled *A Divine Enthyme of true Obedience or a Taske for a Christian*.

Commissioners rule on parish property fraud

1603–1631

Land and houses in the Cliffe, acquired by the Crown at the Dissolution from the Fraternity of St Thomas, were granted in 1591 by Queen Elizabeth to two gentlemen of London, William Typper and Robert Dawe. The properties were transferred in 1603 to the fourteen trustees, known as 'feoffees', of St Thomas's church, either as a result of a purchase by public subscription or else as the gift of an anonymous benefactor, and their 'rents, issues and profits' were to be applied to the support and mainte-nance of the parish church and to 'the relief of the poor who shall, from time to time, be inhabitants of the Cliffe . . .'

In less than thirty years the church had almost lost the lot. By 1631 only three houses and a blacksmith's forge in West Street were producing any profits for the parish.

The two-acre Wish orchard and a garden at South Malling had been acquired by Cliffe grocer Ralph Akehurst, who served as a churchwarden on four occasions. The rector, the Reverend Anthony Huggett, had appropriated a barn and stables in North Street and shared the profits from them with William Waters and churchwarden Robert Palmer. Also in private hands were two houses in North Street and three in South Street, occupied as fif-teen separate units. Even the documents and deeds relating to the properties were stolen from the locked chest in the church in which they were kept.

Evidence of this theft, and the details of the properties the deeds referred to, were given by thirteen parishioners to a com-mission set up in 1631 by the Court of Chancery under an Act concerning Charitable Uses. The commissioners ruled that in future all the rents and profits from the lands must be paid to the churchwardens and they must account for them yearly to the parishioners. And for the next thirty years they did. Until 1667, when Simon Edmunds who had been a churchwarden in 1659 and again in 1662, was made a feoffee. He promptly settled all the church's South Street properties on his daughter, Ann, when she married.

This second fraud went undetected for more than 100 years – until it was spotted by solicitor, Francis Wheeler (see pages 42-43).

When it was a crime to be a single mother

Authority had little sympathy for single mothers in the seventeenth century. When, on 15 December 1634 spinster Joan Alice gave birth to 'a live male bastard' at the Cliffe she was in such distress that she 'strangled him later the same day'. The inquest jury, in returning a verdict of murder, seemed more concerned with the fact that she 'had no goods or chattels, lands or tenements in Sussex' than with her emotional state. She was committed to jail by the coroner and at the assizes pleaded not guilty to murder but was convicted and hanged.

A similar tragedy, but with a less irrevocable outcome, took place on Christmas Day 1650. Susan Hockham, another 'spinster of the Cliffe', gave birth to a live male child 'which by the laws of England was a bastard'. The inquest jury was told that she placed him between two linen sheets 'and did choke and strangle him . . . whereby he died'. No information about the poor woman's state of mind was given but it was made clear that 'she had no goods or chattels, lands or tenements at that time or ever after'. However, someone was on poor Susan's side for at the assizes she pleaded not guilty and was acquitted. 'She had not fled and was therefore discharged, paying her fees,' the coroner noted.

Simply having an illegimate child was a crime for which women were imprisoned.

'1643 October 5/6 Elizabeth Gourd, widow of Hartfield, had a bastard. To be sent to House of Correction at Cliffe' is the laconic entry in the Quarter Sessions Order Book for that year.

The law was kinder to men. Basketmaker Thomas White and his son were fined a mere 1s 2d (5p) in 1645 for poaching fish.

WORK STARTS ON A HOUSE OF CORRECTION
September 1610

Foundations for a new prison to replace the one at Lewes Castle are now being laid on the south side of West Street. The site for this House of Correction – 'between the Red Lion and John Harman's tenement' – was bought in September 1603 for £250 from Robert Emery, a cutler of the Cliffe and Thomas Hodgson, a gunfounder of Framfield. The cash for it was advanced by four county justices, who will be repaid by a tax on householders in the rapes of Lewes and Pevensey.

THE NAME IS THE SAME . . .
16 April 1605

An inquest jury heard today that Robert Emery, 'a shoemaker formerly of the Cliffe' had, on 5 April, attacked Robert Martyn with a knife worth twopence. He inflicted a four inch deep wound from which his victim immediately died. At the assizes Emery pleaded not guilty to murder but was convicted and hanged.

. . . AND THE SAME AGAIN

Was he the Robert Emery who sold 'a tenement, barn, stable, garden and backside' as a site for the new House of Correction in 1603? And the Robert Emery who had four acres of land at South Malling on which was 'a fair dwelling-house, a malthouse and the rest planted with apple and cherry trees'?

This Robert Emery told a Parliamentary Commission that he had leased the land for the past 40 years and spent £300 improving it but the papers he produced were 'so eaten with mice and rats that no date was left therein'.

The Commission noted that Emery was 'a very poor man, hath many children' and relied solely on the profits from the land to feed them.

Benefactor dies before new church is started

John Evelyn was five years old when, in **1625,** he was sent out of London, where the plague was raging and the death toll had topped 5,000 in one week, to live with his grandparents in the Cliffe.

He is a bit careless about dates in the diary, entering against **1627:** 'About this time was the Consecration of the Church of South Malling . . . the building thereof was chiefly procured by my grandfather, to which he left a rent charge of £20 per annum; which likewise I pay'd, till I sold the Impropriation' [which he did in 1648] 'to Mr Kemp and Alcock for £3,000'.

Against **1630** is: 'I was now put to school to one Mr Potts in the Cliff' and 'This year my Grandmother (with whom I sojourn'd) being married to one Mr Newton a learned and most religious Gent'. Evelyn describes his mother, who died in **1635** as 'of proper personage, well timber'd, of a brown complexion; her eyes and hair of a lovely black . . . of rare memory, and most exemplary life'.

26 October 1648
'To Lewes, in which journey I escaped a strange fall from my horse in the dark from a high bank about Chaylie.'

1626

Retired merchant John Stansfield, lay rector of St Michael's at South Malling, died at his home in the Cliffe on 9 March. He was buried in All Saints', Lewes, where his first wife, Elinor, who died in 1613, was also buried. For more than thirty years Stansfield ran a successful import/export business from the Cliffe. Through the port of Newhaven he shipped iron and grain to the West Country and wheat to the South of France in his 50-ton merchantman *Elinor Stansfield,* and imported salt, wine and fish.

When he retired he devoted his time and his fortune to the welfare of the people in the area in which he lived. He was one of the fourteen feoffees of St Thomas in the Cliffe and may well have been the anonymous donor who acquired for that church the houses and land it had once held from the College of South Malling. He certainly played a key part in setting up the charity whereby rents from these lands benefited the church and the poor of the parish.

In July 1623 John Stansfield paid the Earl of Dorset £700 for the rectory and parsonage of South Malling, together with the 'capital mansion and other buildings belonging to the Dean of South Malling in Malling' and three years later he 'gave a yearly pension of £20 for ever to a preaching minister to serve. . . in the church that should be built at South Malling where ye olde one was long since decayed'. He did not survive to see one of its foundation stones laid by his eight-year-old grandson, the diarist John Evelyn.

The restored memorial to John Stansfield, erected by his second wife, Jane, who joined her husband in effigy.

St Michael the Archangel, South Malling, the exterior looking today much as it did when it was built.

Cows, horses and pigs cause consecration confusion

1628–1632

Parishioners of South Malling have petitioned the Archbishop of Canterbury to be allowed to hear divine service and to celebrate the sacraments in their new church without it being reconsecrated.

Archbishop Abbott at first said 'yes' but when he learned that horses, cows and pigs had been stabled and sheltered in the ruins of the old church on the site he changed his mind and issued an interdict forbidding the minister, churchwardens and parishioners from entering the building until it and its churchyard had been reconsecrated. This was done by Theophilus Field, the newly elected Bishop of Oxford, on 24 May 1632.

Money was raised for the new church by collections made in parishes throughout Sussex. A system of 'briefs' – brief appeals by the parson at Sunday services for the congregation to contribute through the collection to specific causes or projects – had been started at the Reformation. Charles II issued letters patent authorising a brief in respect of the rebuilding of St Michael's. The Sunday chosen was 21 April 1628, and the Cuckfield Register of Briefs records that at mattins that day the collection at Holy Trinity 'for South Malling Church, beside Lewes, gathered 8s 9d'.

HORSE HAS A DRINK – AND DROWNS ITS RIDERS

6 July 1619

A drink of water caused the death of William and Abel Rossam, an inquest jury heard today. Both men were riding William Rossam's bay gelding at South Malling when it went to drink from a marl-pit and accidentally slipped into the water which was about 7ft deep. The two riders fell off and were drowned.

WHO WAS TSE?

This gilded weathervane, incised with the date and the initials TSE, was placed on the tower of St Thomas's in 1620. There is nothing in the church records to indicate who TSE was. Churchwardens at the time were Edward Claggett and Henry Hale.

HARVARD MARRIES AT MALLING

19 April 1636

John Harvard, a graduate of Emmanuel College, Cambridge, and Anne Sadler, daughter of the rector of Ringmer, were married today at St Michael's, South Malling. The couple met at Ringmer where John Harvard often stayed with his friend and fellow student at Cambridge, John Sadler, son of the rector and brother of the bride.

Ten months after their wedding the couple sailed for New England. Fourteen months later John Harvard died. His widow carried out to the letter his wishes that half the estate he had inherited from his mother, which amounted to £770, and the whole of his library, should be used to found the college which now bears his name.

IDLE HANDS

15 July 1647

Sarah Sewell, a servant to William Bugg of Cliffe, was today sent to the House of Correction for being 'an idle person'. She will be set to work there and receive due correction until a Justice of the Peace authorises her release.

Churchwardens told: Copy St Thomas's Communion Rail

4 July 1635

A number of injunctions about the content of services, the layout of churches and suitable dress for the clergy were delivered on the occasion of a Metropolitan Visitation to Cliffe church. It was conducted by Dr Nathaniel Brent, vicar general to Archbishop William Laud, a stern and uncompromising enemy of all Nonconformists. He ruled that every communion table should be placed at the upper end of the chancel and should be positioned north/south.

'And it should be railed with a decent rail to keep off dogs and to free it from other pollutions' he said, and told churchwardens to take as their pattern the communion rail of St Thomas's, which he described as 'very comely and decent'.

He also ordered that:
a) all clergy should, when outside their houses, wear canonical habits, that is 'coats made with sleeves like unto a Gown.
b) all afternoon sermons should be replaced by catechising and
c) communion was not to be administered 'except to those who kneel'.

The visitation, which began at Chichester on 27 June, was not all sweetness and light. Dr Brent, who had suspended four rebellious members of the congregation for refusing in open court 'to bow at the blessed name of Jesus' questioned Messrs Bunyard, Maynard, Russell and Gyles so effectively and at such length that 'late at night they all submitted' and agreed to observe the law of the church and persuade others to do likewise. He did not have as much success with Parson Jennings, whom he had forbidden to preach for 'particularising in the pulpit', and calling one of his parishioners an 'arch knave'. Jennings replied that 'it was a lively application' but the parishioner had misheard, thought he had been called a 'notched knave' and fallen out with the barber who had trimmed him.

Another matter that caused Dr Brent concern was that Mr Harrison had exchanged his parsonage house at Stanmer with Sir Richard Michelbourne, the lord of the manor. 'It may be justly feared that the church will suffer wrong in a short time,' he wrote in his report. 'He saith it was done by special order of the late Archbishop. I propose to examine the truth thereof (because I do not believe it) before the Michaelmas Term next.'

Distress and destraint for God and king

THE CONVENTICLE ACT OF 1664

In human terms Henry VIII's Dissolution of the Monasteries, certainly in respect of the Cluniac priory at Lewes and the Collegiate Church at Malling, was carried out in a gentlemanly fashion. Admittedly the buildings were dismantled but the occupants were not persecuted.

It was not so when, after the repressive Puritanism of Cromwell's Commonwealth, came the reaction of the Restoration. The Conventicle Act of 1664 banned meetings of more than five people for religious purposes, other than those of the Church of England. And people were encouraged, with offers of cash and a percentage on goods confiscated, to inform on their friends and neighbours.

One of the first magistrates to take action under the Act in this area was Sir Thomas Nutt. He coerced two men, Relf and Goring, to name people attending an illegal meeting at the foot of Mount Caburn on 29 May 1670. As a result, four county justices, of which Sir Thomas was one, convicted the minister concerned and forty members of his congregation 'without sending for them or hearing what they had to offer in their own defence' says Horsfield in his *History of Lewes*. Warrants were issued for the five shilling fines to be recovered by distraint and sale of goods and

Relf and his brother-in-law, Charles Buckland, a churchwarden of St Michael's, South Malling, set out on 1 June to collect them.

It was a chance to cheat and they took it, Relf because he needed the money and Buckland because he was 'sufficiently, though causelessly, prejudiced both against persons and the cause against which he is now engaged'.

Their first call was on John Prior and they took four cheeses from his shop in the Cliffe for his fine of ten shillings. They then went next door to draper Thomas Ridge and took fifty shillings worth of goods from his shop to defray his thirty shillings fine. From Cliffe carrier, John Tabret, they seized a cow he kept on his farm at Malling but the animal made its way back to its field that night and they had to go and collect it again.

The pair then turned their attention to Lewes and the outlying villages and by 2 July they had a quantity of goods – and seven cows – for sale at Lewes market. The animals were knocked down to Sir Thomas Nutt's brother for £14 15s but as he had no pasture for them, he sold them on to one of Sir Thomas's tenants. The same day the rest of the goods Relf and Buckland had seized were auctioned cheaply at the Star Inn.

| CHURCH CONDUCTS IN-DEPTH SURVEY OF DISSENT | Bishops were directed in 1669 to make a speedy inquiry in to how many conventicles were held in every parish; of what type they were (Baptist? Presbyterian? Roman Catholic? Quaker?); the names of their heads or teachers; how many usually met at them; and what sort of person did they attract.

The returns showed Cliffe with one conventicle of an unspecified sect attended by sixty people 'of the middle sort' and South Malling with one Presbyterian conventicle, attended by 'at least 500 people' also 'of the middle sort.' In neither case was the name of the head or teacher given. |
| --- | --- |

Husband chains wife to bedpost

In the Cliffe it was mainly the Quakers who suffered and ministers and members of the reformed church who took action against them. Both sides milked the situation for all it was worth, accusing each other of bigotry, brutality, idolatry, false witness and every single deadly sin they could think of.

Mary Akehurst, neé Baker, was a dedicated follower of the teachings of George Fox and most keen to spread the 'Blessed Testimony and Joyful Tidings of Salvation.' This she tried to do in 1659 by asking awkward questions of the Independent minister at St Michael's-in-Lewes, the Reverend Walter Postlethwaite. She was hauled out of the church and her haberdasher husband, Ralph Akehurst, twice a churchwarden of St Thomas's, was sent for. He took Mary home and 'so punched and pinched her that she could not lift her arms to her head'.

This did not stop his wife from continuing to debate the Quaker cause with the local clergy at every possible opportunity and Ralph's attempts to restrain her became even more extreme. On a warm May day he tied her hand and foot and wrapped her up in hot blankets for five hours. In August he chained her between two bedposts.

with a great chain like a timber chain with thirty five links and a staple and lock, so that the weight of it hath done much wrong to her leg, beside blows and bruises that he hath given her in executing his cruelty in putting on this chain . . .

Mary's fellow Quakers, 'fearful that murther may ensue' delivered an itemised account of her sufferings in a letter to two Justices of the Peace and also pinned copies of it to the door of Cliffe church 'so thereby it might be made knowne unto all'. However, Mary must have made it up with her husband and returned to the marital bed for in 1661 their son, Alexander, was baptised in Cliffe church and three years later another son, Thomas, was baptised there.

Ralph died in 1666 leaving Mary a boat in Brighton, houses in Hastings and £250. She was soon running the family's haberdashery business, issuing her own trade tokens and continuing to further the Quaker cause. In 1670, for holding a meeting in her house, a £20 destraint warrant was issued against her 'and they did take away goods to the value of £29'.

Seven years later Cliffe rector, William Snatt, who vowed 'wholly to root out the name of Quaker about the town of Lewes', issued a complaint against Mary about the non-payment of tithes and she was held in Horsham gaol for fourteen months. The last mention of her in the *Sufferings of the People called Quakers in Lewes* is in 1683 when on 11 August 'Mary Akehurst, widd', and others were each fined three shillings for not attending church on three Sundays. A warrant for their arrest and imprisonment was not executed because of the charge it would have incurred to the Hundred of Ringmer.

WILLIAM PENN VISITS THE CLIFFE

William Penn, the Quaker founder of Pennsylvania, was Mary Akehurst's house guest on 28 September 1672. He recorded in his journal that, after he had been preaching at Mayfield, some 17 miles away, he 'went through wet and dirt safe to Lewes and lodged at Widow Acre's'.

Malling House, built by John Spence in 1710.

The law moves to Malling

1671

There were comparatively few people and even fewer buildings in this large parish at the beginning of the seventeenth century. Farms, crofts, cowsheds were dotted about on the edge of the brooks and slopes of the Downs to the north and east but the buildings that housed the secular canons of the collegiate church of St Michael the Archangel had been dismantled. No longer did the Primate of all England make regular visits with an entourage of chaplains, clerks and cooks to spend weeks or months at his mansion.

In May 1671 the land on which that mansion stood was bought by William Spence, a barrister from Balcombe. He died two months later and it came into the ownership of his brother, John, who was deputy lieutenant for Sussex in 1688. It was his son, also named John, who built the Queen Anne house which, since 1968, has housed the headquarters of Sussex Police.

CLOCK CONTRACT IS SIGNED

1670

Ditchling blacksmith, James Looker, has agreed to make a new clock for Cliffe church, supplying all the materials except the dial, and to keep it in repair for three years, for the sum of £5 10s. It will replace an earlier clock which was repaired in 1650/51 by 'Mr Gorynge of Lewes'.

BRIDGE IS 'GREATLY IN DECAY'

29 April 1652

The wooden bridge which spans the Ouse between the Cliffe and Lewes is 'greatly in decay and in urgent need of repair'. However, it has lasted well since 1563, when the county justices ordered it to be rebuilt at a cost of £87 5s 3d.

The necessary repair work, which will be supervised by surveyor John Chatfield, will cost an estimated £80. This amount will be be shared equally by the inhabitants of the rapes of Lewes and Pevensey.

NEW LEASE ON CLIFFE MILL

1 November 1689

The windmill on Cliffe Hill, together with an acre of ground, has been leased by Sir John Gage to William Comber of Horsted Keynes for a term of twenty-one years at an annual rent of 13s 4d. Sir John has covenanted to renew the lease for a further twenty-one years or pay his tenant the value of the mill and its tackle. If he fails either to renew or repay his tenant can dismantle the mill and move it elsewhere.

'New built' inn named after William and Mary

1690s

When John Hodge 'new built a tavern' in North Street, almost opposite the Dorset Arms, in 1694, he named it the King and Queen to mark the accession of William of Orange and his wife, Mary. The House of Guelph had been offered the throne of England by an assembly of peers and commoners in order 'to save the country from popery and slavery'.

Noncomformists soon found the restrictions imposed by the Roman Catholic Stuarts on their religious observances considerably eased. The Act of Toleration of 1689 virtually gave Dissenting ministers and schoolmasters the equivalent of a 'get out of jail free' card. All they had to do to avoid penalties for attending conventicles and not attending church was to appear at the Quarter Sessions, swear an oath of allegiance to their joint sovereigns, declare that they did not accept the doctrine of transubstantiation, and agree to an amended version of the Thirty-Nine Articles. The form of words they had to sign was:

I do solemnly declare in the Presence of Almighty God that I am a Christian and a Protestant and as such that I believe that the scriptures of the Old and New Testament, as commonly received among Protestant churches, do contain the revealed will of God; and that I do receive the same as the Rule of my Doctrine and Practice.

Section 13 of the Act provided a special declaration for the Quakers. It did not do much for the Roman Catholics, which bothered the inhabitants of the Cliffe and South Malling not a bit.

They remembered all too well the excesses of the Marian persecution and they welcomed the clause in the Act of Toleration that barred a Roman Catholic from ever ascending to the throne of England.

The burning of ten Protestant martyrs in Lewes on 22 June 1557. They are Richard Woodman of Warbleton; George Stevens, William Maynard and Alexander Hosman of Mayfield; Margery Morris and her son, James, of Heathfield; Denys Burgess of Buxted; Mary Groves of Lewes; and the wife of John Ashden of Rotherfield.

3. AN ERA OF ENTERPRISE WITH
TOUCHES OF ELEGANCE

1701–1800

The Cliffe continued to expand commercially in the eighteenth century and shops, inns and business premises, timberyards, tanneries and breweries spread from West Street along South Street, up East Street and along North Street into Malling. Along the banks of the Ouse the wharves grew bigger and busier, handling outward bound cargoes of Wealden iron, timber, wool and wheat and incoming cargoes of coal, salt, seafish and other commodities. There was expansion in life styles and leisure too. Families who had made their money in trade were building houses and planting gardens, and throughout Sussex a professional class was growing up with an interest in creating their own country estates on the fringes of the towns.

Malling offered the Spences and the Russells the opportunity to build fine houses on sites of mansions once occupied by the the dean, the canons, the sacristan and other officers of the dissolved College of St Michael the Archangel. In the Cliffe china dealer and churchwarden Thomas Baldy was creating a magnificent garden; the Lamberts were painting their pictures; Dr John Delap was writing his poems and plays for the London stage; and the inhabitants were learning about electricity from Mr John Rose, perhaps attending a concert version of John Gay's *The Beggar's Opera* at the Bear; watching Mr and Mrs Philip Astley's performing horses at the Dorset Arms – or playing cricket on Cliffe Hill. They were also enjoying the occasional cockfight at the Wheatsheaf and some bull-baiting in the Coombe, as had their fathers before them.

The elegance of Georgian architecture did not extend into the constructional chaos of West Street which had all the disadvantages of eighteenth-century urban life – bad drains, a too narrow carriageway and unhealthy over crowded houses –

> This E V E N I N G, being the 11th inftant,
> *At the* B E A R I N N, *Bridge-Foot*
> # The Beggars Opera
> The SONGs will be SUNG,
> By One who perfonates all the Characters, and enters into the different Humours, or Paffions, as they change alternately throughout the *Opera.*
> The Characters are diftinguifhed by the Modulation of the Voice; and 'tis a certain fpirited Manner of reading an Opera, fo as to entertain
>
> To begin at Seven of the Clock
>
> TICKETS to be had at the BEAR INN; and at the PRINTING-OFFICE; at a Shilling each.
>
> * * * Ladies and Gentlemen intending to favour the *Performer* with their *Company,* are requefted to provide themfelves with Tickets, as no Money can be received at the door.

but one big advantage. It was the only eastern access road to Lewes and its shops and services were assured of a constant stream of customers from the surrounding towns and villages. They struggled with their animals through the narrow thoroughfare, beneath which at intervals ran culverted sewers, to buy or sell at the weekly stock market that from the middle years of the century had moved from the Fair Place to more spacious premises at the top of School Hill in Lewes.

A showplace of the neighbourhood, and one of the county's first newly-created, as opposed to

The 'beauteous scenes' viewed from Baldy's Garden. In the foreground is the Cricketers, an inn well patronised by members of the Cliffe Cricket Club and guest teams after matches on the club ground on top of the hill. The signs above the door bear the name LENEY'S & SONS and, lower down on the left hand sign, is the word ALES .

historically significant tourist attractions, was the Hanging Gardens on the western slopes of Cliffe Hill. The gardens were created by long-serving Cliffe churchwarden Thomas Baldy and originally approached from the garden of his china shop at the bottom of what was then known as East Street. The site today is on the Cuilfail estate and part of it is occupied by a modern white chalet-style house which has the name 'Baldy's Garden' on its gate. The original gardens, and the prospect from them, are described by Thomas Woollgar, who would have seen them at their best and obviously knew their creator, for he says of him:

Mr Thomas Baldy keeps a considerable glass and china warehouse in front of the West Street. He is a very courteous person and a virtuoso in various researches tho' not a Bigot to any particular attachment, and he is ever ready to indulge strangers with the inspection of this delectable eminence, the improvement and disposition of which is entirely the work of his own hands.

Of the gardens Woollgar has this to say:

Here are pleasant winding walks, trees and ever greens of various kinds, flowers of various species, and some of them flourish even in winter when others of the same kind are dead in the gardens of other persons.

There is an arbour sheltered from the prevailing wind, hives of bees, alcoves and seats from which visitors could enjoy the views over the surrounding countryside. In the summer the eye was entertained by the sight of numerous mowers cutting the grass in the brook lands and meadows and by the reapers who gathered the corn on the higher ground. In the winter, when the brook lands and levels were covered with water, the scene represented the perspective of a lake or small sea with little islands in the midst. In frosty weather, beside the glassy surface, may be seen skaters on the ice and gunners after the wild fowl, with other such objects of diversion.

The daughter of Edmund Lund, rector of Cliffe church from 1725–77, immortalised the gardens in gentle, ladylike verse:

The beauteous scenes that all around it smile
Delight our eye and all our care beguile.

Another young woman who visited Lewes twice in 1782 was Mary Capper, the sister of James Capper, vicar of Wilmington. In her diary she describes the garden as 'a very neat spot, laid out with taste and kept exceeding neat'. Mary also visited Malling Deanery, then in the ownership of Sergeant-at-Law William Kempe. She describes its garden, which had been laid out over the filled-in fishponds from which occupants of this former religious house obtained their food on fast days, as: 'remarkable only for its shady glooms fit for retirement and peaceful contemplation . . .'

Alterations made to the river towards the end of the eighteenth century were for commercial rather than for environmental reasons – in fact it probably looked prettier before it was straightened, embanked and its shallows removed. The country was in the grip of canal fever and everywhere riparian landowners were forming companies to promote grandiose schemes for the waterways running through their lands. An Act of 1791 made the trustees of the Lower Ouse Navigation responsible for the river below Lewes and the works they carried out made the nine miles stretch to Newhaven navigable for sea-going vessels. By 1795 two long cuts had been made and the river embanked above Southease. One of them, Cliffe Cut, straightened the river and formed an island off South Street; the other, Pool Bar Cut, removed the loop opposite the chalk pit. The work of removing shoals and making a tow-path along the bank so boats could be hauled along by horses was not finished until towards the end of 1803.

The course and banks of the river and the drainage problems of the Lewes and Laughton levels had been addressed on a number of occasions since 1421, the year in which the special Commission of Sewers was set up to view and repair the banks of the river from Fletching to Seaford. The silting-up of the river's Seaford Head outlet and the creation of a 'new haven' to the west at the end of the sixteenth century had the effect of not only making a deeper, more direct and safer outlet to the sea but also somewhat reduced the flooding of the levels. However, before the new sea outlet was made in 1795 – in almost exactly the same spot at which the Ouse entered the sea during the Roman occupation – the tidal rise and fall had been a negligible six inches at Cliffe bridge. This, together with the fact that there was only a slight seaward slope in the valley floor through which the river meandered meant that the ebb was not fast enough to drain water off the levels and some 6,000 acres of land in the valley remained under water for most of the year.

The improvements undertaken by the trustees on the advice of their engineer, William Jessop, cost £15,000 to put into effect, but achieved their object. They gave the Ouse a tidal variation on spring tides of up to 11ft (3.35 metres) at Cliffe Bridge and 8ft 6ins (2.50 metres) on neaps. The increased speed of flow not only scoured out the channel but had the effect of reducing the time on passage of vessels from Newhaven from five to two hours.

It is not surprising that schemes to improve the roads and waterways, expand the economy of the Cliffe, improve its educational facilities and even introduce a kind of community care were, in the main, confined to the latter years of the century. For from 1710 the inhabitants were doing their best to cope with recurring epidemics of smallpox which caused so many deaths that the Cliffe graveyard had to be extended in 1718 and again in 1796. They were not helped by the weather which, nationally and locally, was appalling. Frosts so severe that the river froze over were followed by floods that ruined the corn harvest and left water a foot deep in St Thomas's church. There was also an earthquake which did little damage and a hurricane which did a lot.

GRAVEYARD IS EXTENDED
1718

The graveyard on the east side of North Street under the overhang of the cliff is now too small for the needs of the parish. Two houses on the south side have been bought for £28 and a trust has been set up to extend the graveyard onto this site.

HEAD COUNT
1717

A new way of conducting parish visitations has been introduced by Archbishop William Wake. Incumbents have been sent a whole series of questions of the 'How many families in your parish?' variety. Cliffe admitted to 101, of which fifteen were Presbyterian, four Quakers and one, an Anabaptist. The rector, John Clifton, added, with reference to the number of communicants: 'About sixty usually receive at Cliffe – if they would come.'

Smallpox: Scourge of the century
1710

An outbreak of smallpox affected more than a thousand people and claimed some 120 lives in the Lewes area in 1710–11. Many of the casualties lived in the overcrowded area of the Cliffe, which had increasingly become a centre for seaborne trade. It was here the outbreak may well have started – introduced by seafarers who had been to the East or Far East where the disease was endemic. There was a second epidemic in the 1730s and a third outbreak in the 1750s. It was at about this time that doctors in the locality began inoculating people at risk with 'infected matter' in the hope that they would have a mild attack of smallpox from which they would recover and therefore be immunised against any future infection.

Those inoculated had to rest indoors, ideally in a specially prepared isolation unit, for the fourteen days until they had recovered, which not all of them did. The survivors would then be allowed to take regular 'airings' out of doors for a further fortnight before rejoining the rest of the community.

Not everyone kept to the rules. Merchants with businesses to run would be out and about in the market place as soon as they felt well enough – very likely infecting everyone with whom they came in contact and so bolstering the case against inoculation about which opinions were deeply held, and deeply divided.

In 1767, when the village of Glynde opted for a blanket inoculation of its inhabitants, the vicar, the Rev Thomas Davies, reported to the lord of the manor, Dr Richard Trevor, Bishop of Durham, that the neighbouring villages of Beddingham and Firle '. . . last night had the impudence to threaten to mob us, whether out of the parish or out of the world I cannot tell'.

JESUIT DROPS ARE A CURE FOR THE AGUE

It was not until improvements were made to the drainage of the Lewes and Laughton levels, breeding ground of the *Anopheles* mosquito, that there was a noticeable reduction in the number of cases of malarial ague in the Cliffe.

Until then sufferers from alternating bouts of shivering cold and high fever had to rely on the ague tincture known as Jesuit Drops to relieve their symptoms. The drops, which were sold by itinerant apothecaries, contained quinine, an alkaloid obtained from Cinchona or Peruvian bark, that had been brought back from South America by Jesuit missionaries – hence the trade name.

The bridge, painted by James Lambert Jr. c1781.

The *entente* is *non-cordiale* as first stone bridge is built

1727

King George's Master Mason, Nicholas Dubois, had just completed the rebuilding of Stanmer House for Henry Pelham when he was commissioned to design a bridge to replace the wooden structure that arched across the Ouse from West Street, Cliffe to Lewes. The demise of the wooden bridge is recorded, with the minimum of detail, by William Ridge in his *Book of Memorandums:*

The extravagance of two churchwardens whose partnership in

> January ye 2: 1726: Clift bridge was drove away being Sunday in the morning.

A decision was taken to rebuild the bridge in Portland stone, which was supplied by builder, Arthur Morris, whose yard was then on the Cliffe side of the river. The following year he moved across to Eastgate. Architect and builder did not get on. Dubois found Morris 'saucy and unruly' and accused him of trickery and dishonesty. Morris called Dubois 'a French son of a bitch'. Their collaboration, such as it was, did not end in tears but in a bridge of great strength and beauty. It had, however, one drawback – the carriageway was only 10ft wide and there was not room for loaded wagons, one going west, the other east, to pass side to side.

BRIDGE TO BE RESURFACED

12 January 1749
An estimate of £29 15s 8d for repitching Cliffe bridge has been accepted by the Quarter Sessions. The work involves taking up 218 yards of the existing pitched surface and laying a new surface.

PECULIAR VISIT

Archbishop Thomas Secker made personal visits to as many of the peculiars of Canterbury as he could between **1758** and **1761**. He found Cliffe church 'small, but neat, especially the altar piece' and 'tolerable, for a small congregation'. Returns showed that of the 133 households in the parish of St Thomas in the Cliffe there were thirty-seven Presbyterians and independents, thirteen Anabaptists, seven Quakers and six low Absenters.

CLIFFE MILL BURNS DOWN

10 March 1760
The mill on Cliffe Hill, which belongs to baker Thomas Cruttenden, burnt down in one hour at 8pm last Wednesday. 'It is not known how the fire started', said the *Lewes Journal*.

Malling Deanery, as it was in the late nineteenth century.
Photo: Bartlett Collection, Sussex Archaeolgical Society.

Family discord at the Deanery

When, at the age of twenty-four, Richard Russell was working as an assistant to his doctor father in Lewes, he had cause to attend William Kempe at Malling Deanery. There he met, and later married, his patient's only child, Mary, much to her father's annoyance. The wedding, in 1719, was at St John-sub-Castro church across the river, rather than at the church a few yards from the bride's home, which suggests that it was a somewhat clandestine affair. Russell then went to Holland to study medicine at the University of Leyden, which had the foremost medical faculty in Europe at that time. He gained his doctorate in 1724.

Religious rather than reasons of social incompatability perhaps accounted for Kempe's disapproval of the match. He was a staunch supporter of the reformed Church of England and, as Impropriator of the benefice of St Michael the Archangel, Malling – an office that came with his purchase of the Deanery from John Evelyn in 1648 – he had sued Quaker Ambrose Galloway for the tithe on two acres of meadowland belonging to the church and

valued at a yearly rent of £3. So, for a debt of three shillings – a tenth of the land value – Ambrose Galloway was 'carried to the gaol at Horsham where he remained about eight weeks.' Richard Russell's parents were both members of the Presbyterian chapel in Westgate and their children, although christened in St Michael's parish church in Lewes were, in the same year, each baptised at the chapel as well.

Kempe carried his antipathy towards Richard Russell to the grave. In his will, made shortly before he died in 1720, he declared that his daughter had married against his 'consent, will and good-liking to the great grief and impairment of the health of her mother, notwithstanding the many and frequent admonitions, arguments and persuasion used by me and her mother to prevail with her to do otherwise'. He ordered that Russell was not to have any interest or power in the trusteeship over the estate inherited by his daughter and that her eldest male heirs were to bear the name of Kempe. Russell was not even to be used as a Christian name.

Writers and artists in residence

In the eighteenth century culture followed commerce into the Cliffe. Two men, born by chance in the the same year, 1725, attained national recognition for their talents.

The Reverend Dr John Delap, poet and playwright, lived in a house on the west side of South Street, part of the site of which is now a small car park. He was vicar of Kingston and Iford, and later Woolavington, from 1765 until his death in 1812 but found time from his ecclesiastical duties to write a number of now forgotten tragedies for the London stage.

His *Hecuba,* with David Garrick speaking the prologue, was performed at Drury Lane in 1761, *The Royal Suppliants* – for which he tried to get Dr Johnson to write a prologue – ran for ten nights in 1781 and *The Captives* was staged in 1786. A book of *Dramatic Poems,* dedicated to Lady Mary Pelham, and printed by W Lee of Lewes, appeared in 1803.

Dr Delap had his admirers. Mary Capper, the sister of Wilmington rector James Capper, wrote in her diary on 8 October 1782:

> I had the unexpected gratification to meet Dr Delap, a man of famous abilities. I cannot say he shone in the topics of the day – the conversation was trivial and beneath his particular attention.

The impression that the reverend doctor was a bit of a bore is confirmed by Fanny Burney, who described him as 'a man of deep learning but totally ignorant of life'. Perhaps that was too sweeping a statement for Dr Delap did, on occasions, show an awareness of local politics. For instance, he immortalised the forty-five Cliffe residents who made their way to Chichester to vote in the 1774 election for a Knight of the Shire, with an ode which begins:

> Such spirit late thy sons inspir'd,
> O Cliffe! With British ardor fir'd,
> When, leagu'd in friendly, firm array,
> To Chichester they bent their way.

and in 1792 he published a satirical ode denouncing Thomas Paine for promoting radicalism in his book, *The Rights of Man.*

James Lambert, described by his brother, John, as 'stationer of the Cliffe', was both an artist and musician. He was organist at Cliffe Church from the age of twenty until his death in 1788, playing, for an annual salary of £5, the instrument on which the churchwardens lavished so much  money. He also compiled a hymn book for use at St Thomas in the Cliffe and other churches.

His contemporary, Paul Dunvan, in his *History of Lewes,* says of Lambert:

> As he advanced towards maturity he received some instructions from a music master; but in painting he had still to trust solely to his own taste and application; and with such means his proficiency in landscape became truly admirable.

Just how admirable were his paintings is evidenced by the award of a prize of fifteen guineas by the Society of Artists (later the Royal Society of Arts) in 1769 for the best original landscape painted on canvas and the Sussex topographical views commissioned by antiquarian Sir William Burrell in 1775 for a history of the county which he was compiling. The book was never completed, but Sir William appreciated Lambert's landscapes enough to bequeath them to the nation.

NOT SO OLD
BONES

NOT SO OLD BONES

19 June 1749

Bones of a human body, thought to be that of a young woman, were found last week by a man digging flints on Cliffe Hill. Buried nearby was the ferrule from a walking stick and the buckle from a woman's girdle.

'The position of the body and its burial on the hill a foot beneath the surface gives rise to the belief that the woman was murdered,' says the *Lewes Journal*.

PACED OUT

3 May 1753

William Ridge has paced the distance from the top of Malling Hill to Lewes market house. Going by way of 'Dr Russell's bridge' near Malling Deanery, he made 2,240 paces in 26 minutes.

It was a shorter walk via Cliffe bridge – 1,840 paces in 21 minutes.

GOOD CATCH

12 November 1760

Two pike, one weighing 27½lbs and the other 31lbs were caught on one draw in the Ouse by 'Counsellor Kempe's people'. The 31-pounder measured 4ft from nose to tail, and was sent to Sergeant Kempe who was in London.

Market and fairs are lost to Lewes

1753

When new houses were built to the north of the church to form St Thomas's Square the Fair Place, site of the charter fairs and weekly market, was reduced to half an acre. As a result the October sheep fair was moved in 1747 to Trayton's field at Old Malling and later on to the Paddock, a site owned by Henry Shelley, in Lewes.

The spring fair for black cattle continued to be held in the Cliffe but six years later the weekly Wednesday market also moved across the river. Cliffe traders, furious at what they considered to be an encroachment on their chartered rights by the setting up of a daily market in Lewes, decided in 1755 to take proceedings against its owners. However, they were dissuaded from doing so when they took counsel's advice and were told they had little hope of succeeding with their planned suit.

The Fair Place, without the sheep, was as busy and bustling in May and at Michaelmas as it had always been. There were plenty of itinerant traders crying their wares; jesters and tumblers entertaining the crowds; and sideshows displaying marvels and monsters. It was from here that Gideon Mantell bought an alligator which had died from the cold and sent it to Guy's Hospital to be preserved.

The October sheep fair prospered on its new site. In 1776 there were 15,000 sheep offered for sale, the largest number in living memory. Prices were high in 1784 with wethers from 24s to 27s, ewes selling for 18s and lambs from 12s to 14s 6d. The following year there was double the number of sheep and prices were low. One lot of fine ewes for which 16s was refused on the morning of the sale sold later at 13s each.

Cliffe's market house originally protruded into West Street from the east entrance to the Fair Place but when the road was re-pitched and the pavement repaired in 1779 it was set back in line with the rest of the buildings on the north side. Its removal caused some minor damage to the house next door which was repaired at a cost of £2 18s 1½d. Over the years the room above the market house was let by the churchwardens for various purposes but there is no mention in the accounts of any expenditure on repairs and maintenance. So, not surprisingly, it deteriorated and in the early 1800s it was taken down.

Founder of Brighton is buried at Malling

1759

When Dr Richard Russell returned to England in 1729 he moved with his wife, three daughters and three-year-old son, William, into Malling Deanery. It was there that he wrote the work that was to make him, and Brighton, famous.

In *De Tabe Glandulari,* which was published in 1750, he made a case for the benefits to health of sea bathing and the drinking of sea water. Three years later he had so many patients taking his cure at Brighton that he decided to move there.

Richard Russell died on 21 December 1759 while on a visit to London and was buried in the Kempe family vault in St Michael's church, South Malling. On 14 August 1764 his widow, Mary, died and was, at her own request, buried in lead and laid to rest 'near my dear and well beloved husband'.

A memorial tablet was placed in the church some years later, possibly by Henry Spence of Malling House. It bears the quotation from *Iphigenia in Tauris* that appears on the title page of *De Tabe Glandulari:*

θαλσκ χλνζε παυτα ταγθρωπου κακα

'the sea washes away all the ills from man'.

Beneath the tablet, left, is a much smaller one showing a horned goat from the Stansfield arms, which are blazoned: 'Vert, three goats passant argent, armed Or'. Its presence is a mystery for there is no blood relationship between John Stansfield and the Kempes and Russells. Their only link is their respective ownership of Malling Deanery.

It was not until a full year after the death of his father that William Russell, then aged thirty-three, obeyed the last wishes of his maternal grandfather and took the name of Kempe.

PARISHES PLAN TO BUILD A PEST HOUSE

27 February 1758

Cliffe and South Malling are to join forces to build an isolation unit for people suffering from smallpox. St Thomas in the Cliffe parishioners intend to borrow 'upon annuity or annuities for life or lives' the cash required for the project, a plan of which is to be produced in a fortnight. The pesthouse is to be built on a site in South Malling parish that is a safe distance from habitation – under the chalk cliffs on the east side of the southern end of South Street.

Churchwardens' spending spree costs parish £550

1748–65

office continued without interruption for seventeen years, cost St Thomas at Cliffe a total of £552 11s 10d in lost revenue.

Andrew Tasker, a hatmaker, and Thomas Baldy, a china merchant and keen gardener, were born nine years apart – Thomas Baldy in 1710, and Andrew Tasker in 1719. Both had continued their respective family's close association with Cliffe church where Thomas's grandfather and Andrew's father had also been churchwardens.

Between 1748 and 1765 they saw to it that the church had a new porch, new pews, a new organ, a new weathervane, a new altar-piece and new windows onto the High Street. The parishioners were quite happy about the additions and improvements. So much so that thirty of them, including a Mr Wheeler, each subscribed one shilling to the vane account and the vane, when it was put up by Mr Pratt at a cost of 4s 6d in 1756, displayed the initials of the churchwardens – AT and TB.

It was not until this Mr Wheeler, (solicitor and county coroner Francis Wheeler) had cause to refer to the parish accounts on another matter (see page 32) that the profligate spending of the two churchwardens came to light. What seriously worried him was the £76 12s 5d that had been spent on 'repair and addition to ye organ twice' in 1755, plus a further £39 'for playing the organ this year and various items.' The usual annual payment was £5.

The feoffees took counsel's opinion and Sergeant-at-Law William Kempe advised that the use of the money of a public charity for such purposes as repairing the organ and paying for an organist and organ blower was 'improper'.

The accounts prepared by the two churchwardens have a curious innocence about them. Two shillings for 'beer to encourage the masons to make haste to finish the first street window' and another two shillings given 'to men for drink that brought the altar-piece from the bridge to the church', is hardly the stuff of premeditated fraud. Thomas Baldy adds, for the accounts are in his writing, 'cannot find what I paid for the bringing of it from Newhaven'. There is no mention of profits from the church estates except the cryptic statement, dated 5 March, 1761: 'Accounts allowed from 1747 to 1761'. Presumably the parishioners simply took their churchwardens' word that all was in order. And so did Archbishop Thomas Secker. On a visitation in 1761 he commended 'the decent, neat and well-judged condition of the church fabric and the careful management of the church estate' – adding that 'such trusts all too often are sacriligiously perverted'.

Reports of what happened next vary. Horsfield in his *History and Antiquities of Lewes* (1835) says:

The parishioners having at length awakened from their blameable supiness, were anxious to investigate the accounts of their confidential officers; but this was boldly refused them by the men in power . . . The sum of £552 11s 10d was on this occasion lost to the parish by a system which cannot be too strongly reprobated . . . that

Cliffe church in 1790,
viewed from the Great Sewer.

of permitting churchwardens or overseers to retain their offices from year to year until they become masters of the parishioners they were chosen to serve.

Paul Dunvan, whose *Lee's History of Lewes* was published in 1795, puts all the blame on Andrew Tasker, describing him as 'one of those oily knaves who are the bane of any place where they can creep into authority'. When proceedings were taken against the churchwardens: 'Tasker for some time found means to evade the stroke of justice and in the end his poverty rendered it altogether useless to proceed against him'. He died in 1767 but the 'indolent, besotted' Thomas Baldy remained a churchwarden until his death in 1782. He was buried at St John-sub-Castro church in Lewes, and left his entire estate, including the gardens he had created, to his partner in the china business, John Lambert, brother of landscape artist and Cliffe church organist, James Lambert.

THIRD CHURCH PROPERTY FRAUD EXPOSED

By chance, in 1770, that eagle-eyed solicitor Francis Wheeler discovered that St Thomas's had a long dormant title to some houses in South Street – the ones that 100 years previously feoffee Simon Edmunds had handed over to his daughter on her marriage (see page 24). Wheeler found that recently they had been leased for twenty one years to Charles Bunting by John Goring. He managed to trace Goring to Greenwich, where he was living as a pauper, and persuaded him to forgo any claim to the properties. He then negotiated for the feoffees to buy back the remainder of the lease from George Bunting, as the cheapest way of recovering the houses.

In the taverns of the town

The old alehouses of the Cliffe that had offered rest and refreshment to the traveller and slaked the thirst of bargemen and farm workers, were beginning to look for more customers in the second half of the century.

Some, like the Wheatsheaf which was opened at the bottom of the hill in Malling Street in 1783 by Benjamin Hearnden when he retired from teaching, catered for the pedlars, drovers, and farmers coming into town for the fairs and markets. Others sought a more regular and moneyed clientele.

In 1767 Quaker John Rickman, who owned the Bear by the bridge, bought its adjoining stabling from cutler William English for £30 and set about extending his hotel premises. When he died in 1789 and was succeeded by his eldest son, Richard, the Bear Hotel had become a centre for the wool trade of Lewes and a place for balls, soirees, anniversary banquets and travelling entertainments. These included such oddities as insect acts. Bee-charmer Daniel Wildman, who could 'command Bees out of the Hive into his hat or any person's in the company' appeared there and patrons also had the chance to see a 'live SEA DOG taken on Monday, February 13th, as it was sleeping between two Rocks, near *Beachy Head*'.

Another inn that provided accommodation and entertainment as well as ales, wines and spirits and midday dinners for the cricketers who played on Cliffe Hill was the Dorset Arms. It was known as the Catts because the leopard supporters of the arms of the Earl of Dorset on its inn sign looked to the locals like *felix domesticus*. It had an auditorium and for Signor Marco's Troupe from Italy

admission charges were: 'Pit 1s, first gallery 6d; upper gallery 4d'. The prices were lowered to sixpence, fourpence and threepence for 'Curious Experiments of a Camera Obscura'.

Across the road was the King and Queen, advertised in 1764 when it was offered for rent, as 'an old accustomed house with good stabling, brewhouse and other conveniences'. There, in 1776, was 'Miss Hawtin from Coventry'. A handbill describes her act:

> This little artist, or phenomenon of human nature, by the help of her toes and feet only, is capable of many curious performances. She threads a needle, . . . sews, picks up pins, feeds herself, drinks out of a glass with ease and exhibits sundry other fancies too tedious to mention.

It concludes, in very small print:

> Ladies and Gentlemen are left to their own generosity; children and servants threepence each.

Another 'extraordinary Production of Nature' to appear at the King and Queen was:

MARGARET MORGAN
THE SURPRISING
Monmouthfhire FAIRY

An undated handbill describes her as 'the greatest Curiosity ever exhibited'. It goes on:

> This amazing Part of the Human Species was born at *Magar*, in *Monmouthfhire*, is now in the feventeenth Year of her Age, strait and well-shaped in every Respect, is only 31 Inches high, and weighs but 18 Pounds, which is 3 inches fhorter, and 8 Pounds lefs in Weight, than any Woman ever fhewn to the Public before.

The Swan in West Street, an old established house, tenanted by someone called 'Reynoles' in 1633 when it was willed by John Edwards of Cuckfield to his son John, closed it doors in 1788. Shortly afterwards the King and Queen's name was changed to the White Swan.

Education becomes organised

33 Cliffe High Street – formerly the Swan Inn, a girls' school and John Button's Classical Academy.

Whatever schooling the boys and girls of the Cliffe and South Malling had before the Reformation was monastic, or from tutors in their own homes. The first to offer organised lay education in the Cliffe was the parish clerk, George Beard, who rented the room above the market house as a classroom from 1750.

Benjamin Hearnden advertised his Cliffe boys' boarding school in the *Sussex Weekly Advertiser* in August 1769, offering:

Writing in various hands now in use. Arithmetic thro' all its branches, both practical and theoretical. . . merchants accompts . . .any branch of measuration . . .

but giving no details as to its whereabouts. Two years later he was appointed master of Mayfield school and was seeking someone to take over his Cliffe school and the writing master's job he held at a 'Young Ladies Boarding School'.

Mrs Elizabeth Symonds' girls' boarding school opened 'opposite Mr Woodgate's in the Cliffe' in May 1782. Fees were fourteen guineas a year and the girls were taught English language grammatically and instructed in every branch of useful and ornamental needlework and embroidery. The following year she announced that her husband William Symonds intended to open a boys' school 'where he will teach English, Writing and Arithmetic'. In 1788 Symonds advertised that he had 'engaged a proper assistant for his

school' and was limiting the number of boarders to six 'at reasonable terms.' Too reasonable, perhaps, for Symonds, whose other business interests included bookselling, auctioneering and paperhanging, had his estate and goods sold at auction in 1793 to satisfy his creditors.

The Cliffe gained a prestigious academy of learning in 1796 as the result of two disasters. Five years previously John Button had, at the age of twenty-nine, opened what he later styled as Button's English Classical Academy at 86 High Street, Lewes. In 1794 he was having bigger premises built in a field near St Anne's church when, on 6 October, the framework was blown down by a high wind. The builders absorbed a £40 loss and started again, only to have the new building gutted by fire.

For two years Button rented premises in All Saints parish before moving to 33 West Street which had, until 1778, been the Swan Inn and, from 1793 had accommodated Mrs Ann Chaffin's girls' boarding school. When the house was rebuilt around the turn of the century and given its present bay windows, John Button bought the freehold.

WEDDING GIFT

20 October 1779

For no known reason, other than that he was married there, Benjamin Vauder-Gutch of Brook Street, Grosvenor Square, London has presented Cliffe church with an oil painting of the Ascension. Or perhaps he did so because his bride in 1776 was Miss Sophie Egles, niece of churchwarden Robert Plumer.

PRISON HAS A WHIP-ROUND

17 December 1782

Penal reformer John Howard today visited the House of Corrrection in the Cliffe. The prison, rebuilt in 1740 by Joseph Daw, is an outpost of the county jail at Horsham and, says the *Lewes Journal,* 'beggars are rounded up and brought there to be whipped with suitable severity'.

Chapel's congregation comes under attack

1775

A meeting house with seating for 600 has been built 'on a piece of ground belonging to Mr Thos. Davey, Surgeon at the bottom of the lane leading up Cliffe Hill' (now Chapel Hill). On 13 August it opened for religious worship under the patronage of Selina, Countess of Huntingdon, widow of the ninth earl. She had been converted to Methodism by her sister, Lady Mary Hastings, and spent her energy and fortune on building chapels in Brighton, Tunbridge Wells, Bath and other fashionable resorts in the hope of attracting members of the upper classes to the churches of her Connexion.

Her chapel was not welcome in the Cliffe. The fifty-nine founding members had their services disrupted by 'indecent noise and clamour and by flying stones and bricks against the walls thereof and lighted combustibles within the house, interrupting the congregation at their devotions and putting them in fear of their lives'.

After the attack came a rival attraction. The new rector of St Thomas's church, Richard Cecil, turned out to be such a spellbinding preacher that the chapel's congregation deserted to his services in droves. The deserters even tried to close down the chapel from which they had defected but it was kept open by the efforts of a determined few and for a time visiting ministers were supplied by the Countess from London and the seminary she had set up at Tredecca in North Wales.

In 1780 the elders decided to appoint their own pastor. They chose twenty-seven-year-old Tredecca-trained Joseph Middleton from Brighton, a believer in adult baptism involving total immersion. Unfortunately for the chapel's future, there was a faction in its congregation, headed by Robert Smith, which firmly believed in infant baptism. A battle of beliefs raged for the next three years in spite of attempts by moderates on both sides of the baptismal schism to unite the parties in 'Christian affection'. It ended in July 1784 when Smith and his supporters gave the chapel's trustees

The meeting house in Foundry Lane.

an 'either he goes or we go' ultimatum. Middleton complied with a request to hand over the key and with a handful of adherents moved to Puddle Wharf, which had been vacated by the Quakers. The following year he became minister of the little wooden meeting house that his fellow Baptists had built in what was to be called Foundry Lane. He was succeeded at the Countess of Huntingdon's chapel by Jenkin Jenkins, a believer in infant baptism and also an ardent Francophobe who managed to collect £70 from members of his congregation for the war against the 'Satanic French Republic'.

Jenkin Jenkins

There was nothing controversial about Jenkins' ministry until he came under the influence of William Huntington, a forceful preacher and writer of religious tracts. This bastard son of a Kent farmer had moved to Surrey after getting a local girl pregnant and it was while pruning a pear tree in a garden at Sunbury-on-Thames that he had 'a vision of Christ all stained with blood'. It convinced him that he was one of God's elect and he set out on a mission of soul-saving which brought him hundreds of devoted followers. They built a chapel for him in London but the Redeemed Coalheaver, as Huntington styled

William Huntington.

himself, did not confine himself to the capital. It was when preaching in Maresfield in June 1792 that he met Pastor Jenkins. Soon he was offering his new friend spiritual comfort and naming him 'the Welsh Ambassador of God's Truth', for he took great delight in finding elaborate names for his disciples as well as for himself. However, the Coalheaver's attempt to take over the chapel and impose his beliefs upon its congregation met with fierce resistance and at the end of the century his disciple, the 'Welsh Ambassador', was forced to leave and pursue his ministry elsewhere.

This second schism was the beginning of the end of the Connexion in the Cliffe. After Jenkins' departure there were a few visits by some ministers from London and then the chapel closed – to reopen again to yet more upsets and a third parting of the ways.

SUNDAY SCHOOLS
13 February 1788

The idea of a one day a week charity school in each parish for 'the education of poor children resident in Lewes and its environs' was approved at a packed public meeting at the Star inn today. People subscribed generously to a central fund from which individual parishes could draw to set up a school. However receipts from a benefit performance of *The Merchant of Venice* on 21 December 1789 in the theatre in St John Street were disappointing. The charity event had been suggested by Lord Eardley, a generous subscriber to the cause. He and Lady Eardley had driven over from Brighton and they arrived at the theatre preceded by six running footmen, dressed in white. That was possibly the high spot of the evening. Certainly the 'gentleman of the town' who addressed the audience about Sunday Schools had a poor notice from the *Lewes Journal.* It was deliverered, it said 'in a tone of voice too low for us to hear. . . we can only say he made his exit to applause'.

Note: The first Sunday School in the Cliffe was opened in 1808 in the Countess of Huntingdon's chapel in East Street.

New drainage plan for the Lewes levels

1769–1777

There were a number of schemes put forward for improving the 'all flood, no flow situation' on the Lower Ouse in the eighteenth century.

The river was the main artery for trade between the hinterland of mid-Sussex and the rest of the country, but there was an insignificant fall in height from Cliffe Bridge to the sea outlet at Newhaven. This meant that all too often goods being shipped to the coast were delayed for days as the loaded barges grounded in the shallows.

Flooding was also a major problem and in 1766 John Smeaton, the designer of Eddystone lighthouse, was asked to prepare a scheme for the sewering and draining of the levels up to the river's then navigable limit of Barcombe. He proposed channelling the drainage floodwater from above Hamsey, mainly along the west side of the river, to join what he termed 'a mother drain' on Rodmell Tenantry Brooks. Drainage channels from Kingston to the north-west and from the Laughton levels across Ranscombe Farm to the north-east would also lead into the mother drain and be taken, via a 'great 12 foot tunnel' under the Ouse near Stock Ferry to a new sea sluice at Newhaven.

Unfortunately for future generations little of his well-planned scheme was built. Between 1769 and 1777 the river was widened in places at a cost of £1,700 but it was not until 1795, when the entrance to the harbour at Newhaven was deepened and its piers extended, that work started on William Jessop's plan for improving the navigation, initially up to Lewes and then for a further twenty-two miles to Lindfield.

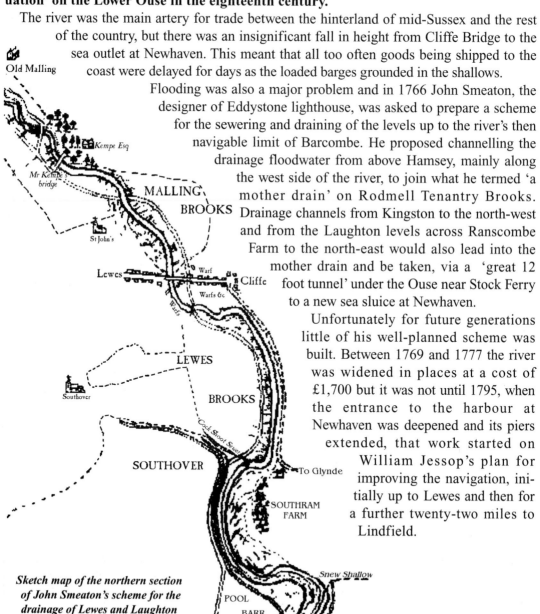

Sketch map of the northern section of John Smeaton's scheme for the drainage of Lewes and Laughton levels.

The world's oldest cricket ball – from a match on Cliffe Hill?

1775

Twelve years before the MCC was founded by Thomas Lord in Dorset Fields, Marylebone, the Cliffe Hill Cricket Club was pulling the public – and the punters – to its pitch in a natural ampitheatre on the Downs above South Street. On 24 July 1775 the *Sussex Weekly Advertiser* announced that:

> On Monday next a Match of Cricket will be played . . . against Ninfield-Stocks and Hooe, for 5s 3d each man and £20 the match.

In the same issue readers were informed that:

> This day a great match at cricket will be played on Cliffe hill; between the married men and batchelors belonging to the Swan club in the Cliffe.

It could well have been a ball from this match, or others played on Cliffe Hill, that was discovered two centuries later when old plaster was being removed from an inside wall of 17 South Street. The cache included two women's shoes of a pattern dating from 1760-1770, two smaller balls and an early type of bedroom slipper.

The cricket ball, which weighs 3½ozs, is perhaps some fifty years older than the one in the museum at Lord's. When it came up for sale at Christies in June 1995 it was bought for £843.75 by Nicholas Sharp, a Surrey resident but a keen supporter of Sussex cricket. Writing about his purchase in the *Cricketing Memorabilia Society Magazine No 28* he says that he showed the ball to the works manager of Dukes, a firm that has been making cricket balls since 1760, who considered that it was made by a local cobbler, perhaps for his son or the son of a customer. Its cover is of cowhide and the inside, which is visible through a split along a seam, is mainly of cobblers' thread wound round and round to form a sphere.

In the early 1770s cricket was governed by the first known laws of the game. There were only two stumps, 22ins high, with a single bail 6ins long. The third stump was not added until 1776. Cricket bats had a curved blade and were huge and heavy. All bowling was underarm and along the ground and cricket balls were expensive – a top quality ball costing as much as seven shillings. The 1744 laws stated that: 'Ye ball must weight between five and six ounces'. However, this would presumably have applied only to matches on which large wagers had been laid – and there were occasions when the ball was dipped in water if it was found to be underweight.

LEG BREAK? BUT THERE IS A SPARE TO HAND

12 July 1790

An entirely new definition of the term 'leg break' was revealed to SWA readers today. Apparently a young man 'amusing himself at cricket' in Coombe Bottom, had the misfortune to break one of his legs. A manufacturer of those articles was sent for and, on arrival, took off the broken limband replaced it with a new one 'which enabled the young man to pursue his diversion to the end of the game.' Too tall a story? Or was the leg that was replaced a wooden one?

EARLY START FOR FAIR DAY SESSIONS

9 May 1791

The Recorder, Sergeant Kempe, will take the chair at the Quarter Sessions at 9am – an hour earlier than usual – on Friday.

He is doing so, he says, as it is Cliffe Fair Day and he wishes to discharge the Grand Jury, and others whose attention the court may require, as 'expeditiously as possible'.

CLIFFE SAYS IT WITH FLOWERS

12 July 1792

The people of the Cliffe have a pretty way of welcoming distinguished guests – they strew their path with flowers.

Visitors so honoured often reward the strewers. Certainly the Archbishop of Canterbury, John Moore, did so after confirming at Cliffe church three days ago. He was in a generous mood, and gave two guineas to 'some poor old women who strewed him'.

In 1771 Prince Ernest of Mecklenberg-Strelitz 'regally tipped' those who threw flowers before his feet as he made his way from the White Hart Hotel to view the prospect from Baldy's Garden.

Turnpikes add to the traffic chaos

1782

When the road-building Romans left around AD410 little was done in Sussex, or elsewhere, to maintain their metalled roads or make new ones. Wherever possible, the movement of goods was by water rather than overland, which was all very well if the departure and destination points followed the north/south run of the river. Loads going east to west or west to east had to take their chance over steep gradients of slippery downland chalk and muddy marshland to arrive at Cliffe bridge which, until a draw-bridge was built at Newhaven in 1784, was the most seaward road crossing of the Ouse.

Tinkers tramped from town to town, buying here and selling there. Everyone else used horse power – or oxen if the load was heavy and the weather wet. Farm wagons bringing produce to the weekly market; carriers with one-horse drays; the six-, four- or two-horsed carriages of the gentry; and possibly a cartload of prisoners for the House of Correction had to squeeze along the narrow West Street and, if going to or coming from Lewes, struggle across the 10ft-wide Cliffe bridge. Road traffic to and from the north had to climb or descend the 1,000ft-high Malling Hill or make a 500-yard detour towards Malling House and rejoin the road at Stoneham.

Until trusts were set up under the Turnpike Acts to construct, metal and maintain specific sections of road, parishes were responsible for repairs to the routes through the area under their control. A few appointed surveyors and tackled the task with some degree of efficiency but in many cases it was a haphazard affair with forced labour being used to patch up the worst bits. It was in 1752 that the road was turnpiked from the Malling boundary through Uckfield and Nutley to Wych Cross and this had the effect of bringing even more traffic into the chaos of the Cliffe.

The southern turnpike was built in 1759 from South Street past Beddingham, Glynde and Firle to Alfriston, where it joined the old road over the Downs to Eastbourne. It was extended in 1792 from Bo-peep over Chilver Bridge and east to join what is now the A22. Tolls on the turnpikes were steep. A carriage drawn by six horses had to pay 1s 6d (7½p) at the tollhouse before the barred gate would be opened for it to pass through on to the road; one drawn by two horses ninepence; and by one horse sixpence. Cattle cost a penny a head, sheep twopence a score – pedestrians walked free.

'Strangers' gatecrash the smallpox inoculation

January 1794

When Lewes decided to follow the example Glynde had set in 1767 and order a general inoculation, people from outside the area daily poured in to take advantage of it. They were not welcome and on 20 January 1794 Lewes, Cliffe, Southover and Malling residents met to see what could done to deter them. Nothing, apparently, except call a halt to the inoculation, which had started the previous week. It was agreed that its continuance would, by the 'Introduction of Strangers, be injurious to the Trade &c of the Gentlemen who had undertaken the Business of Inoculation'. Eight unenforceable resolutions were passed at the meeting, not one of them detailing the consequences of non-compliance with their terms.

Prior to the general inoculation medical practitioners from outside as well as within Lewes were happy to offer their services to anyone in need of them. Dr George Saunders, originally based at Chailey Common, assured readers of the *Lewes Journal* of 14 April 1770 that he employed the 'SUTTONIAN SYSTEM' upon which it would be 'needless to expatiate'. He then proceeded to expatiate for almost half a column about the 'Blessing of the Discovery' which had saved many thousands and concluded:

> I beg now to recommend myself to the attention of your County in general, and if my poor Endeavours reach to the saving of the meanest Individual, the Feelings of a humane Heart will amply repay those Labours, which shall ever be directed to the public Welfare, and the Preservation of domestic Tranquillity.

Dr Saunders rented Lamb House in East Street (Chapel Hill) from the painter James Lambert Jr, and lived there while he attended to the inhabitants of the Cliffe. He inoculated 500 of them 'and they all survived' he announced on his return to Chailey. Lewes surgeon, Joseph Ridge, had a more commercial approach. On 21 June 1773 he announced that, with Thomas Davey, he had taken a house on the Broyle and it was open for the reception of patients. He advertised his terms for treatment as 'five guineas each Person, accessory accommodations provided. (Tea, Sugar and Wine excepted.)'

In all about 2,290 local people and some 600 'strangers' were injected with smallpox in the Borough of Lewes, Southover, Cliffe and South Malling in January 1794 and forty-six of them died.

TIDE CARRIES BODY FROM OUSE TO WORTHING

11 February 1792

The body of a Cliffe bargeman who drowned in the Ouse was washed up six weeks later on the beach at Worthing. It was presumed that Tera Galten had accidentally fallen from the barge he was poling along the river for his quant pole was found standing up in the mud near Stock Ferry and the barge floating a considerable distance away. The *Lewes Journal* reported on 24 March that the body was identified 'by the initials of his name tattooed or stained with gunpowder on one of his arms'.

A MOTHER – AT FIVE MONTHS

June 1792

An 'uncommon instance of early gestation' has occurred in the herd of Mr Grover of the Cliffe. One of his cows dropped a fine bull calf which was only fourteen months younger than his dam. 'Which circumstances will convict the forward mother for have intrigued at the age of five months', comments the *Lewes Journal*.

The poor will be working from home

23 March 1797

The Cliffe is at last about to acquire a workhouse of its own. It was unanimously agreed today, at a public meeting of the inhabitants and parishioners of St Thomas in the Cliffe, that a 99-year lease on church land in South Street should be granted by the feoffees, at a yearly rental of £6, to fifteen trustees 'for the purpose of erecting a House of Industry to employ the poor people who now, or shall be, inhabitants of the Cliffe'.

A week later these trustees formally granted a 21-year lease to Charles Freeeman and Thomas Davey, in trust for the churchwardens and overseers of the poor who will be responsible for the new workhouse. The yearly rent of £37 10s and the cost of maintaining the building are to be met from the poor rate.

The Cliffe has had a long wait for a workhouse. It was on 20 April 1735 that a public vestry meeting decided that one was needed and agreed to meet again in a fortnight's time to settle where, and in what manner it was to be built.

That meeting was never held, or if it was, it was not minuted. Not until April 1766, when it was agreed at a vestry meeting that Widow Rowland 'be put in the workhouse except she will provide for herself', was a workhouse mentioned again. A possible explanation is that the pesthouse for smallpox victims, built jointly by Cliffe and South Malling at the far end of South Street in 1758 (see page 41), later became a shared poorhouse.

However, the parish did provide a health service of a sort and some discriminatory community care. The inhabitants present at an Easter vestry at the Swan in 1772 presumably had their reasons for ruling 'that the Widow West shall not be allowed clothes' and that the Widow Eager was not to be allowed 'any pay for the future'. However, they did agree that clothes should be provided at the discretion of the overseer for 'Pilford's children'.

They were in a more generous mood the following year when Samuel Grover had the misfortune to break his leg. He was allowed seven shillings a week for himself and his family and when he was better he was to be 'relieved discretionately as the overseer felt proper.' His father, 'being an encumbrance and burden to the family' was to be immediately removed from them – presumably to the shared workhouse.

And what of the weather?

1701–1800

Earthquake shocks, lightning strikes, gales, floods and a frost so severe that it was possible to walk across the Ouse by the bridge were among the extreme weather conditions experienced in the eighteenth century. They were carefully recorded by William Ridge in his *Book of Memorandums.*

'A hundred barns, four mills and a great many chimneys, hovels and trees' were blown down in 'a terrible high wind' between 10am and 8pm on 8 January 1734 and on 25 October earthquake shocks were felt in Lewes between 3am and 4am 'but did no damage'.

In the winter of 1739-40 there was a severe frost, with occasional thaws and heavy falls of snow, from 23 December until 21 April. Farmers started ploughing around 23 February 'but could plow no depth and there was a vast many plows broke . . .' The tidal Ouse was frozen so solidly by the bridge that people could walk across it on the ice.

The river was again iced over at the beginning of 1776 and on 28 January bargemen, out of work because of the weather, carried a boat with its sails set through the streets of Lewes and the Cliffe to raise money for food to feed their families. They received a 'liberal contribution' from the inhabitants.

There was serious flooding in the second half of the century. Wet weather ruined the corn harvest in 1768 and on 21 September water flowed up and into the coffee house on the Lewes side of Cliffe bridge. The flooding persisted until 3 December when there was 'A Flood that flowed in every lower room of the Bear and about half way up the Iron Ring that hangs on the warehouse on the North East corner of the Bridge . . . Suppose almost to be as high as at any time'.

On 15 January 1772 the *Lewes Journal* reported a very large flood occasioned by a great quantity of rain that fell the day before. 'I remember that the Flood was so high that a boat swam around the Bear Inn adjoining the bridge' says Thomas Woollgar. There was more heavy rain in November 1773 and flood water came up over the ring and staple on the north east corner of the bridge and up to the tenth brick below the coping stone at the corner of the Bear.

There were two fatalities as a result of the bad weather, both occurring in a severe thunderstorm on 25 May 1784. Lightning strikes killed a bull belonging to Sergeant Kempe and a horse in farrier Edward Tooth's Malling Street stables.

RECTORY IS IN RUINS

November 1799

St Thomas's rectory, in North Street opposite the Swan, is so dilapidated that it is to be demolished and replaced with three tenements. The conversion will cost an estimated £2,000 for which the rector, the Reverend Thomas Aquila Dale, will be responsible 'although' notes the vestry accounts 'he received nothing in the way of dilapidations from his predecessor, Richard Cecil.' Which is perhaps not surprising as this popular evangelist contracted a rheumatic complaint when he was at the rectory and had to give up the living. Dale plans to invest £400 of the Queen Anne's Bounty the parish is to receive for the loss of its parsonage in 8¼ acres of land in Landport Lane.

'SALMONS' IN THE OUSE

1800

The *Sporting Magazine* is concerned that nets with meshes small enough to catch a sprat are in daily use on the Ouse where, in the last few years there have been 'a great number of salmons'. The writer urges the water bailiff to stop the use of 'these destructive engines on the finest river in the kingdom'.

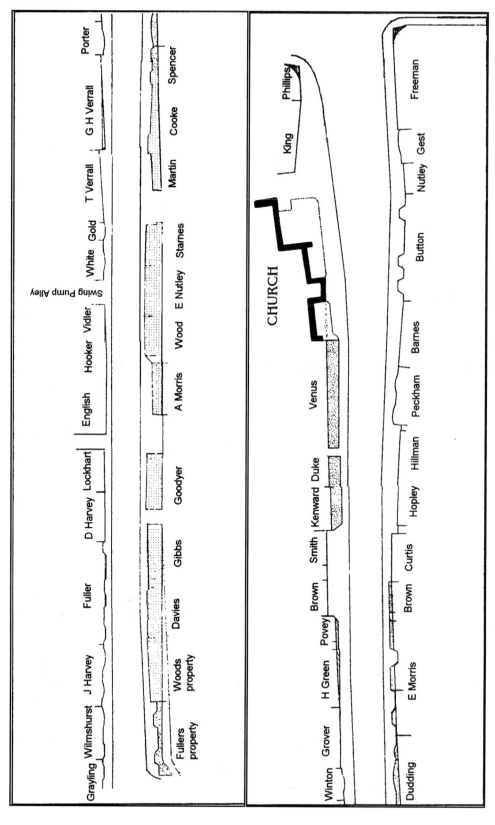

A sketch map, in two sections, of Cliffe High Street going east from the bridge, showing the occupants of the properties, and the 1827 plan for widening the carriageway to a maximum of 25ft by setting the buildings back.

4. Improvements — and an end to independence

1801–1900

The completion of Jessop's scheme to improve the navigation of the Lower Ouse in the early years of the nineteenth century brought immediate benefits to the inhabitants of the Cliffe and Malling. The Lewes and Laughton levels were no longer under water for four or more months of the year. Instead a well-designed system of drainage brought seasonal inundations from the Downs across the flood plains of Malling and Lewes Brooks into the straightened and much faster-flowing tidal Ouse.

Cliffe residents stopped alternately shivering and sweating from attacks of ague. They had, as a result, more time and energy to seek other ways of improving their environment and standard of living.

The water supply was first on the list for attention. A parish pump was erected in 1804 near the church porch to bring water from the well on Chapel Hill. It was paid for out of the poor rate. Two years later, however, both Cliffe and Southover declined to join Lewes in seeking to present a Bill to Parliament for the paving, lighting and cleaning of the streets of the borough and its adjoining parishes.

The next major undertaking was in 1831 when West Street, by now more usually referred to as the High Street, was widened. This £3,000 scheme came about as the result of a plan by the borough and the trustees of the Lewes and Uckfield turnpike roads to divert traffic away from the narrow confines of the Cliffe by making a new entrance to the town. It was to run from Earwig Corner across Malling brooks and over the river by a bridge to the bottom of North Street, Lewes. Had it been built Lewes may well have been spared its present daily rush hour traffic chaos. But it was not to be. The possibility of losing the lucrative custom they had enjoyed from the northern and eastern parts of the county prompted the traders of the Cliffe to take action.

On 27 September 1827, three days after the Borough of Lewes had decided to apply to Parliament for an Act empowering it to build the new entrance road and bridge, a packed meeting at the Dorset Arms, under the chairmanship of George Verrall, subscribed £815 to a fighting fund to oppose it. They did so with the Cliffe Improvement Act of May 1828, under the terms of which the width of the High Street was virtually doubled to 25ft by setting back the premises on the south side and clearing the clutter of buildings round the church. At the same time the turnpike trustees agreed to re-route the steep and hazardous road over Malling Hill to Ringmer and Uckfield on to much the same line that it follows today.

POPULATION TABLE

The population of the Cliffe and South Malling rose in almost every decade throughout the century as this table shows.

Year	Cliffe	Sth Malling
1801	1,113	348
1810	1,258	443
1821	1,362	620
1831	1,408	705
1841	1,545	646
1851	1,477	730
1861	1,820	716
1871	1,991	677
1881	1,664	732
1891	1,559	743

However, it was improvements to the river far more than to the approach roads that brought increasing prosperity to the Cliffe and South Malling in the first half of the nineteenth century. From their wharves in 1810 a fleet of twenty-nine barges carried cargoes of coal, timber, wool, grain, chalk and stone up and down the Lower Ouse and ten barges worked the upper reaches.

An iron foundry had opened on the river bank south of the bridge and it, together with the ship-building industry, provided the jobs that were no longer available to the inhabitants in the surrounding countryside where agriculture was becoming less labour intensive as farmers began replacing men with machines.

It is significant that at this time the majority of employers, educators and administrators in the Cliffe and South Malling were, almost without exception, Non conformists. Iron founder Ebenezer Morris – a descendant of Lewes martyrs Margery Morris and her son, James, of Heathfield – was chairman of the trustees of the Calvinist Jireh Chapel. John Button, headmaster of the academy which he moved to 33 Cliffe High Street in 1796, was a Radical Baptist as was his son, William, who succeeded him. Merchants and shipbuilders Richard Peters Rickman and Burwood Godlee were Quakers, as were Sarah Rickman and Mary Ann Speciall who ran the Lewes Girls' Home in South Street. Days of wine and roses were not for them. Hard work was, and they expected and encouraged their fellow citizens to share their enthusiasm for it.

When they were not at work, or in church, chapel or meeting house, they would be performing some civic duty or attending dinners – either the formal sort held to honour a distinguished visitor or the fund-raising functions of friendly societies and similar organisations, most of them held at local inns.

They had a fondness for fireworks as well as food. The Guy Fawkes night festivities were regarded by members of the newly-formed Orange Lodges and ultra-Protestant groups not as a celebration of the failure of the Gunpowder Plot but of the rescue of England from the rule of Rome by the landing of William of Orange on 5 November 1688. As a result of their interest and support the festivities became more organised, more political and incited more religious rancour.

Other outdoor activities were of a sporting nature. Cockfighting and bull and badger-baiting were banned in 1849 but went on, clandestinely, in the Coombe. Cricket continued to be played on Cliffe Hill but gave way to golf when a course was set up there in 1897. The Lewes Rowing Club, formed in 1871, had its slipway and clubhouse on the east bank of the river, off South Street.

The handsome entrance gates to Morris's iron foundry would have been made on the premises. Behind the foundry are the gas works.

And it was in South Street, on the morning of 27 December 1836, that there occurred the only avalanche so far recorded in this country. Tons of snow crashed down from the cliffs and demolished the cottages of South Malling's parish poorhouse, killing eight people and injuring a further five.

Fifty-six years later, an eye-witness account of the disaster was issued by Lewes councillor James Pelling and his wife in the form of a Christmas card – a surprising and insensitive way of marking the festive season. The account was a virtual reprint of a pamphlet that had been published in 1863 and dedicated to the memory of:

THOSE WHO SUFFERED

FROM THE

Lewes Avalanche

in 1836

AND THE

INHABITANTS OF THAT TOWN

WHO SO NOBLY GAVE THEIR SERVICES ON THAT OCCASION.

When a copy of the Pellings' card was received by Miss Frances-Ann Thomson at her home in Polegate she wrote at once to the *Sussex Express* which, at her request, had printed 300 copies of a pamphlet giving an account of the sad event from the manuscript of her late father, William Thomson. He had been at the scene and was chairman of the committee set up to raise funds for the survivors and relatives of the victims.

'I would wish to be informed if it is quite the correct thing for any one else to make use of, or publish such without consent of those to whom the copyright belongs?' she asked.

'There are still residing in Lewes and its neighbourhood some of my late father's friends and relations, to whom I shall be most happy to forward (on application) a copy, one of which has been accepted and lodged in the British Museum.'

Her letter was published and with it a footnote from the editor assuring her that the persons who had reprinted and circulated the pamphlet without her consent had committed 'an act of literary piracy'.

In 1881 the Cliffe and part of the parishes of Southover and South Malling were incorporated into the borough of Lewes. The Cliffe opposed the takeover for a number of reasons. It was administered efficiently by the Duke of Dorset's manor of Ringmer and by the Cliffe Commissioners; it benefited considerably from its church charities; it had its own fire brigade; had widened its main street; had decided by a nine to six vote it did not want a police force; and had insisted on organising its own celebrations for the coronation of Queen Victoria.

The inhabitants, who had managed their own affairs since Saxon times, petitioned against losing their independence – but without success. On 22 June 1881 a Royal Charter of Incorporation was proclaimed and, together with part of South Malling, the Cliffe was brought, quietly screaming, into the borough of Lewes.

WATER STARTS A FIRE
1801

Flood water started a fire in Swing Pump Alley (now North Court). It came into contact with a quantity of unslaked lime that had been stored in a building there. The lime blazed fiercely but the outbreak was soon brought under control.

TROUBLE AT MALLING MILL
1803

On 5 September a grinder at Malling mill fractured his skull when the twist tackle fell on him. Some years later his brother became entangled in the mill machinery and had to have his hand amputated.

The operation was performed by Dr Gideon Mantell who noted in his journal: 'On my arrival I found a poor boy with his hand dreadfully lacerated; thought it necessary to remove the forefinger and thumb at the wrist joint.'

It was the mill that came off worst in the spring of the following year.

'It cast a swift on its meeting with a cow that was grazing near, who suffered little or no hurt,' reported the *Sussex Weekly Advertiser.*

Iron foundry gives a name to a lane

1801

When coal and iron deposits were found in close proximity in the north of England at the end of the eighteenth century the iron industry of the Weald collapsed. The fires in its furnaces went out, the steam hammers were silent and the farmers, who had become iron masters and cast cannon to arm England, went back to the land. It hardly seemed the right time to start an ironworks in the south, and one to which all the raw materials would have to be brought from a distance. But that is exactly what ironmonger Nicholas Polhill did in a garden he had bought by the river – in what became Foundry Lane.

He opened an iron foundry and workshops on the site in 1801, and for a time it was the only one in the county. Much of the iron he used had been cast in the Weald in the form of firebacks, andirons, agricultural implements – perhaps even the odd cannon. He recycled it and bought a shop in the High Street to display the architectural and domestic articles he was making. Nicholas died in 1811 and James Sturt took over the foundry. Nine years later he too died and Ebenezer Morris, who had been brought up as a farmer, bought the business on the advice of his grandfather. It was run by trustees while the new owner spent ten months in an ironmonger's shop in Newgate Street, London, learning the trade.

Morris took over in 1821 and the business prospered. It soon became apparent that he needed larger premises to display his products so when the Cliffe Improvement Act came into force, instead of adjusting the frontage of the old shop, he demolished it and build a new one.

The foundation stone of 41 Cliffe High Street was laid in May 1828 and in November Morris gave what he described as a 'roof-rearing supper' to the nineteen men working for him and thirty personal friends. A bushel of punch was brewed in the copper kettle that used to hang on a bracket outside the old shop and shared amongst the company 'which did not separate till the early hours of the morning'.

Invasion threat call
to Arms

1803

With Napoleon's army poised for attack across the Channel, Parliament ordered a general mobilisation of local militia forces. The Levy 'en Masse' Act required lists to be made, parish by parish, of men between the ages of seventeen and fifty-five from which a number would be selected for two hours a week military training and would be required, in an emergency, to serve anywhere in the country. However, if enough men volunteered to fight the French the Act would not be enforced. Encouraged by such stirring ballads as:

Britons, to Arms! of Apathy beware,
And let your country be your dearest care:
Protect your Altars! guard your Monarch's throne,
The cause of George and Freedom is your own!
What! shall that England want her sons support
Whose heroes fought at Cressy – Agincourt?

thousands volunteered.

The advantage of expressing a willingness to serve rather than taking a chance on being called up was that each volunteer would get a uniform allowance and be compensated in cash for attending training, exercises and annual camp.

St Thomas in the Cliffe and South Malling came within the southern division of the Rape of Pevensey for which a target figure of 910 had been set. It was later revised to 960. There were 217 names on the list for the parish of St Thomas in the Cliffe and among the sixty-nine noted as 'willing to serve' were four schoolmasters – John Button and his son, John Jr, Henry Roscorla and John Smith – together with six members of the Verrall family, among them upholsterer George Verrall who enrolled in the Sussex Guides, and four Hillmans. Lameness was the most frequently listed health problem and it was noted that sieve-maker John Butcher was subject to fits. 'Infirm' appears in the remarks column beside eight names in South Malling militia list. 'Willing to serve' appears beside six – the churchwarden of St Michael's, George Philcox; four more members of the Hillman family, all of them bargemen; and John Farncombe, a farmer who enrolled himself and his horse in the Voluntary Cavalry.

When Napoleon withdrew his army from the Channel coast and marched into Germany in 1805 the volunteers decided that the emergency was over. All their enthusiasm for part-time soldiering faded away, as did their attendance at Sunday drill sessions. At about the same time the government reduced the training and uniform allowances with the result that, one by one, the various proud voluntary troops of artillery, cavalry and infantry were disbanded.

In 1806 the government made it official and stood down the militia.

Dissenters build a third chapel

1805

Chapel building was a growth industry in the late eighteenth and early nineteenth centuries. When Jenkin Jenkins' ministry at the Countess of Huntingdon Connexion's chapel on Cliffe Hill was brought to an end by the trustees because of doctrinal differences he was soon able to find another pulpit.

He and his mentor, William Huntingdon, at once set about raising funds for a new meeting house and a plot of land on the west side of North Street was bought in 1804 for £420 from Thomas Attreeall.

In a matter of months South Malling builder James Berry had put up a timber-framed structure with a brick foundation on the site. Its east and north walls were faced with mathematical tiles made at Keymer, one of which, near the side entrance, still bears the impression of a cat's paw.

Berry's receipt to Joseph Morris, the appeal fund treasurer, is dated 16 November 1805 and acknowledges payment of £1,754 10s 10d – 'being the limit of Bills of different Workmen for Building the new Chapel in the Cliff, Lewes for the Revd Mr Jenkins.'

Above the round window over the pillared entrance porch was placed a stone tablet bearing the words:

JIREH CHAPEL ERECTED BY J JENKINS WA WITH THE VOLUNTARY CONTRIBUTIONS OF THE CITIZENS OF ZION ANNO DOMINI MDCCCV

'Jireh' is derived from Jehovah-jireh, meaning 'the Lord will see, and provide', the name given in Genesis 22:14 by Abraham to the place where an angel intervened as he was about to sacrifice his son, Isaac.

The interior of the Jireh chapel showing the tall pulpit from which preachers addressed their congregations

The 'Citizens of Zion' were those from the locality who, together with members of Huntington's Providence Chapel in London, had subscribed to the new building. It was formally handed over by Jenkins in 1806 to trustees as:'A place for public worship for Protestant dissenters of the Calvinistic persuasion'.

Jenkin Jenkins died on 2 September 1810, aged fifty-nine, and was buried in a massive stone tomb in the garden at the back of the chapel. The interment was conducted in silence for he had left written instructions that 'nothing be said over me at the vault except my good friend the Doctor should happen to be there and feel inclined to speak'.

His good friend was not there. Huntington was an emotional man and avoided, whenever possible, delivering funeral orations, particularly if the person concerned was one of his friends. However,

The 16ft-long, 10ft-wide and 4ft-high tomb in which the Welsh Ambassador and the Coalheaver were interred at silent ceremonies. Behind the tomb is the Sunday School which was built in 1875.

ALL HANDS TO THE PUMP
1804

The Cliffe now has its first public water supply. A pump drawing water from a well in Chapel Hill was erected near the church porch in October and is now in constant use.

Its popularity has caused problems. The clanking of the handle and the sound of water slopping into the chancel disturbed Sunday services in the church. The feoffees solution was to lock the pump handle so it could not be used at the time of Divine Service but this caused a near riot and it was quickly unlocked and the pump moved away from the porch to the east end of the church.

he did feel inclined to speak about Jenkins at the Jireh chapel on 23 September, until his feelings overcame him – 'I don't like this. I can't bear it,' he said.

Two years later it was his turn to be buried in silence beside his friend, a crowd of 2,000 accompanying his funeral cortege from Tunbridge Wells. He wrote his own epitaph, adding S S – 'Sinner Saved' – as a form of ministerial qualification, and it is inscribed on one of the five slabs on top of vault.

> HERE LIES THE COALHEAVER WHO DEPARTED THIS LIFE JULY IST 1813 IN THE 69TH YEAR OF HIS AGE. BELOVED OF HIS GOD, BUT ABHORRED OF MEN.
> THE OMNISCIENT JUDGE, AT THE GRAND ASSIZE, SHALL RATIFY AND CONFIRM THIS TO THE CONFUSION OF MANY THOUSANDS;
> FOR ENGLAND AND ITS METROPOLIS SHALL KNOW
> THAT THERE HATH BEEN A PROPHET AMONG THEM.
> W.H.S.S.

The Jireh chapel was enlarged in 1824 and a well-appointed vestry added behind the pulpit. From it the resident or visiting preachers would make their entrance and treat the congregation to hour-long tour de force sermons on sin and salvation. Jenkins' successor, John Vinall, another of the Coalheaver's converts, was a particularly eloquent speaker and easily filled the 1,000-seater chapel on Sunday after Sunday from 1829, much to the envy of the ministers of other churches and chapels in the vicinity.

The pump in the metal casing that replaced the original wooden one in 1830.

Victory lights shine out from the 'hanging rock'

November 1805

The summerhouse 'on the hanging rock called Baldy's Garden on Cliffe Hill' was decked with coloured lights to celebrate Nelson's defeat of the combined French and Spanish fleet on 21 October at the Battle of Trafalgar. The illuminations 'produced an effect peculiarly beautiful,' reported the *Sussex Weekly Advertiser* in its county-wide account of the celebrations.

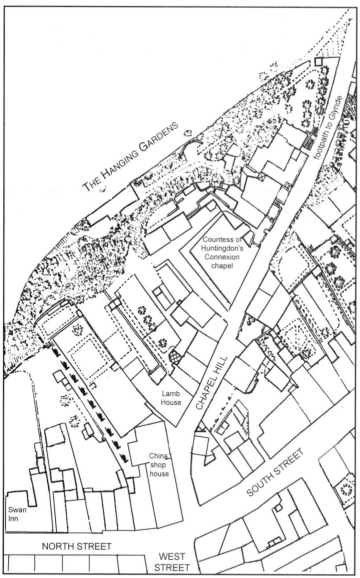

A conjectural map of Chapel Hill with the original access to the gardens indicated by 🐾 🐾 🐾 . Later access was through an iron gate and up steps after the last house on the hill.

The light show had been arranged by George Beard Hoey to whom the gardens had been left by the painter, James Lambert Jr, who died in 1799.

James, the nephew of the senior James Lambert, the Cliffe church organist and the artist responsible for the Burrell Collection of Sussex landscapes, imposed certain conditions to the bequest in his will, of which he made three versions. In the last one, dated 1798, he describes Hoey, founder of the family's plumbing, painting and glazing business, as 'my faithful servant' and leaves him three houses in the parish of South Malling together with 'my pictures, drawing books, other furniture, household furniture and other property' as well as:

. . . that piece or parcel of ground commonly known by the

name of Mr Baldy's pleasure garden with all the buildings, seats, trees, (etc), and after his decease to his son George Hoey Jr. on condition that they or either of them shall keep up the aforesaid pleasure garden in a decent manner as has been heretofore practised.

In an earlier version of his will Lambert describes Hoey as a coachpainter and also leaves to him, and afterwards to his son, 'the garden which has lately been usual for the use of the china shop house', on condition that they keep it in repair and let the people who usually visit it continue to do so. It was in this shop that the creator of the Hanging Gardens, glass and china merchant Thomas Baldy, and his partner John Lambert, James junior's uncle, had their business. And presumably it would have been here that visitors paid 'a modest gratuity' and passed through to what Thomas Woollgar described as 'a gradual ascent raised by the proprietor to the Gate of the Gardens'.

In the will he made in 1795 James Lambert Jr also leaves Hoey 'the messuage in the East Street of the Cliffe commonly called the Lamb House' which had been built in 1716 by John Baldy, father of Thomas Baldy who designed the Hanging Gardens. In an earlier, undated version, he left the 'china shop . . . with adjoining premises etc and with the brick courtyard with right of road into East Street of the Cliffe. . .' to his cousin, Sarah Lambert, and repeated this bequest in the final 1798 version in which he leaves Lamb House not to George Hoey, but to another cousin, Ann Michell.

Lamb House in Chapel Hill . Beside the front door was a stone inscribed: ^{S}/JB 1716 – a reference to John Baldy and Sarah Verrall, who were married at Southover in 1709.

George Beard Hoey had set up as a plumber, painter and glazier at 5 North Street around 1780 and, in his old age – he was the oldest inhabitant of the Cliffe when he died, aged eighty-nine, in 1847 – he lived there with his eldest son and joint legatee, George Hoey, who was then dealing in china and glass from the premises. His second son, Francis, had transferred the plumbing, painting and glazing business to larger premises in Cliffe High Street. Third generation Hoeys, George and Edward, formed the firm of G and E Hoey, plumbers and painters, using Lamb House, then in their possession, as a workshop and store, as had Thomas Baldy in the eighteenth century.

THAW BRINGS FLOOD

29 January 1814

The highest flood within living memory was on Saturday night, after a sudden thaw of the snow that had fallen on the previous days.

The belfry of Cliffe church was flooded to a depth of more than one foot and in consequence there was no service the following day. Floodwater was so deep outside the Wheatsheaf Inn in Malling Street that a boat was needed to carry people across to higher and drier ground.

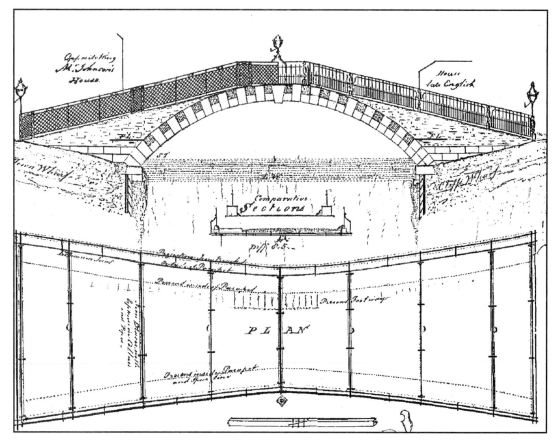

Cater Rand's 'Design'd Sketch for the Improvement of Lewes Bridge'.

Add-on pavement to widen Cliffe bridge

April 1808

The too-narrow 10ft-wide carriageway of Cliffe bridge is to be widened by the addition of an overhanging pavement on the north side and by replacing the wide stone parapets on both sides with 2ft 3inch high cast iron railings.

Tenders for the work, which the county justices require to be completed by mid-August, have been received from Cater Rand in the sum of £798 18s 9d and from Latter Parsons' firm, Molineux, for £749. The latter, being the lowest tender, was accepted. As on previous occasions the cost will be shared between the inhabitants of the rapes of Lewes and Pevensey.

The work involves taking down the present parapet walls, removing the pavement and a 92ft length of carriageway – 46ft each way from the centre of the bridge – and rebuilding and relaying them to a specified width and depth. This will bring the total width of the bridge up to 24ft and the width of the carriageway to 18ft 5ins.

THE MILL THAT CAN KILL

3 January 1813

Taking a short cut home across the enclosure on which Malling mill stands cost 'a poor woman named Wood' her life. One of the sails struck her arm and shattered the bone. Before she could scramble out of the way the next one crashed into her, breaking her collar bone and one of her thighs. She died of her injuries at her home a few days later.

The miller at the time was Henry Peckham. He had taken over the mill from his father, also Henry, who had been declared bankrupt in 1810. It was this second Henry who re-built and modernised the mill and, after the accident to Mrs Wood, raised it by six feet and added an additional floor to the original roundhouse built of Sussex flint.

Residents complain about soap factory's 'offensive smell'

1816

Complaints about the smell from Thomas Evershed's soap factory have resulted in the firm being brought before the court for causing a nuisance. The factory, which was opened in 1811, is behind the Jireh Chapel, two of the leading members of which, Thomas Hooper and his wife, Mary, said in evidence that the smell from it was 'most offensive'.

The Hoopers, who live near the factory, are devoted friends and disciples of Jenkin Jenkins and William Huntington. All four have asked to be buried in the same vault in the chapel garden. An exchange of soul searching letters on the subject of salvation was conducted between Mary Hooper and Huntington. She called herself Philomela, 'the Nightingale', and he signed himself Noctua Aurita, 'the Listening Owl'. The entire correspondence was published in the eighteenth volume of the Coalheaver's collected works.

PARISH OPENS A POOR BOOK

17 September 1815

The vestry has decided to keep a 'poor book'. It will list the name, age and sex of every person taken into the House of Industry in South Street and include details of when and how they were admitted; and how they left – 'whether by death or other cause.'

UP TO THE MINUTE

1817

A minute hand has been added to the clock on the tower of St Thomas's church by William Hooker, clockmaker, of 12 Cliffe High Street.

STATE LOTTERY

Tickets for the State Lottery are on sale in the Cliffe at the premises of James Lambert, Bookseller and 'Mr English's cutler's shop' on the corner of English Passage.

'SPLENDID ILLUMINATION' MARKS QUEEN CAROLINE'S VICTORY

14 November 1820

The withdrawal of the Bill of Pains and Complaints by which George IV hoped to divorce his unconventional but popular-with-the-people wife, Caroline, and strip her of her royal status was marked today with what discoverer of dinosaurs, Gideon Mantell, described as a 'splendid illumination'.

'I never remember seeing one so general,' he wrote in his journal. 'With the exception of the Quakers every house was lighted up in the Town, the Cliffe and Southover. At nine o'clock the fireworks became very general'.

Yards build ships for the coastal trade

*c*1820-1860

For several decades before a railway system was established in the area the merchants of Cliffe and South Malling had added shipping to their business interests. The improvements brought about by the Lower Ouse Navigation Act had resulted in many more barges being built, repaired, loaded and unloaded at the wharves along the canalised Great Sewer to the north of Cliffe High Street.

With the removal of Tapsfield Shallow from the river in 1838 the launching of larger vessels from yards south of the bridge became a possibility and the following year the *Lewes Castle*, the first sea-going ship to be built in the town, was launched by Quaker Richard Peter Rickman and his partner Burwood Godlee from a slipway on the west bank of the river by the Viper warehouse. The *East Sussex News* said of the occasion:

> Saturday 2 March was a fine day and by noon the heights of the Cliffe were crowned by a great number of spectators and the streets empty, shops deserted and all life and animation of the town centred on the banks of the river which, from the cliffs, presented a continuous silvery line covered with apparently diminutive boats decked with pennons of every tint and hue. . . The vessel was christened by Mrs Johnston to cheers from the banks . . .

There was a dinner at the Star at 4pm for more than forty guests at which the proposed toast was:

> The *Lewes Castle*, may she make prosperous voyages and have profitable freights.

The 75-ton ketch *Mary Ann,* built in 1843, was the first keeled vessel to be launched from Charles Wille's timberyard wharf – and the occasion was celebrated with a cricket match in the Coombe. On 28 February, five years later, 'laden with wheat', she was wrecked off Rotterdam. The next vessel launched from Wille's yard was the James Berry-built 182-ton brigantine *Harriett* and on New Year's Day 1866, Edward Chatfield launched his flat bottomed 185-ton topsail schooner *Wallands* from the Bridge wharf.

Several Cliffe residents owned coastal traders. Jeweller and silversmith William Tanner had the 188-ton brig *Olato;* coal merchant William Pannett the 227-ton snow *Conflict;* and the Hillmans owned the *Galway Lass* that sank off Flamborough Head in 1875 with the loss of all hands.

Shipbuilding in Cliffe Cut ended almost as suddenly as it started. It had used Wealden oak but the demand was now for iron ships and Sussex no longer had an iron industry – it had gone to the coalfields of the north.

The launch of the **Lewes Castle,** *with people on every vantage point watching the vessel enter the water from Rickman and Godlee's yard by the Viper warehouse. Her owners were Lewes grocers Edward Monk and Thomas Johnston; Cliffe provision merchant John Farnes; and William Lidbetter.*

The **Wallands** *was built by timber merchant Edward Chatfield for his own use. She was a flat bottomed, schooner-rigged vessel, 78ft in length and with a 9ft 6ins depth of hold. She took timber to the north of England and returned with coals and is believed to have carried the last cargo of tree-nails to the Baltic.*

The **Harriett** *had her hull partly stove in when she was driven by a gale onto the Sunderland coast in 1850. She survived that catastrophe but in 1893, when on passage from Newhaven to Sunderland in ballast, she was one of thirteen ships lost off the Yorkshire coast in a violent storm.*

In dry dock

When the river was straightened by the Cliffe Cut the loop of its original course round the island was retained and the narrow channel running parallel to South Street did duty as a dry dock.

Pictured in the dock is an unidentified snow – a vessel distinguished from a brigantine by a trysail mast aft of the main mast. It has been variously identified as the *Halifax*, owned by Cliffe coal merchant John Hillman, which was there in 1839 for a refit and the following year sailed from Newhaven to Swansea and back in a record eight days; as the 199-ton Sunderland built *Lewes Lass* of Newhaven; and as the *Eagle* – there to be fitted out after her launch in Lewes in 1863.

The same scene around the turn of the century – without a ship in the dock.

New entrance road plan angers Cliffe traders

1827

An entirely new entrance to the town from the east is being planned by Lewes council in conjunction with the trustees of Lewes and Uckfield Turnpike roads. Its purpose is to avoid the difficult and dangerous approach via Malling Hill and the narrow main street of the Cliffe.

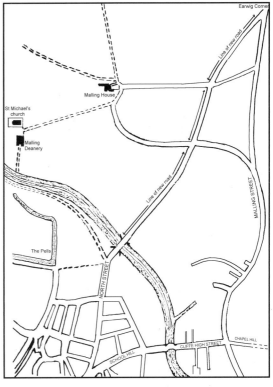

The proposed road would run from Earwig Corner, over Malling Brooks and cross the river by a new bridge and enter Lewes at the bottom of North Street. Also under consideration was a scheme to circuit Malling Hill to the west, so reducing the gradient, and continue to route traffic through the Cliffe. On 24 September 1827 the trustees met and decided on a new road across the brooks.

It was a decision that could mean ruin for the majority of the traders in the Cliffe who have for centuries relied for custom on passing trade from the north. On 27 September six resolutions opposing the new road were passed at a packed meeting at the Dorset Arms. Angry residents argued that there was no public demand for an alternative route – the only people who wanted it were landowners with property on the line it would take.

A four-man committee comsisting of John Farnes, George Verrall, Ebenezer Morris and John Godlee was elected to find a solution to the problem. It decided that the Cliffe must put its own house in order and widen its High Street. Properties, mainly on the south side, would be set back by up to 9ft feet to give a road width of 25ft; some 3ft would be taken off the houses at Cliffe Corner and the house and shop outside the church entirely removed. The cost would be in the region of £3,000, entailing an increase of a shilling in the £ on the rates.The committee was pleased to report that 'the parties are willing to give up what is required, on receiving a fair compensation'.

Also in the Cliffe Improvement Act, which became law on 9 May 1828, was a clause requiring that all future buildings should be no less than 15ft from the centre of the roadway. Lewes immediately abandoned its plan for a new road and in 1830 the trustees rerouted the Ringmer turnpike round Malling Hill, reducing the gradient by some 55ft.

CLIFFE MAKES TOWN'S GAS

1822

The gas that fuels the lamps of Lewes is manufactured in the Cliffe. The Lewes Gas-Light Company was set up on 12 September, with coal merchant Burwood Godlee as its superintendent and Ebenezer Morris its clerk. The works are on the river bank below the bridge and, according to the company's prospectus, they produce inflammable air and gas from coal and other materials and also prepare and obtain 'Coke, Coal-Tar, Pitch, Asphaltum, Ammoniacal Liquor, Essential and other Oils, and other Products.' Horsfield, who published his *History of Lewes* two years after the works opened, was impressed with the process.

'There is nothing more indicative of the progress of science . . . than the application of this aeri-form liquid,' he wrote. 'The gas produced is of a very superior quality. owing to the improved means of purification, by means of quick lime . . .

Some inconvenience has been experienced by the breaking up of the pavement in every direction but this was a temporary evil, which already is nearly remedied.'

Up and away on Fair Day

1828

Travelling balloonist Henry Green brought the crowds out on 22 September, the day of the Michaelmas charter fair. Some 10,000 watched from Cliffe Hill and another 5,000 from other vantage points as the brightly-coloured balloon rose from the gas works, after some delay, and floated away on the south west wind. The delay was caused by lack of lift, either because of the quality of the gas or flaws in the varnish coating of the balloon itself.

Green was airborne for nearly an hour before landing in a field near Deanlands Wood, north of Ripe. That evening, at the theatre in West Street, Lewes, he gave a fulsome account of his flight to an appreciative audience.

A week later he was airborne again from the gas works, this time at the instigation of William Button, who had succeeded his late father as headmaster of the English Classical Academy in the Cliffe. This ascent was made with a passenger, Mr W H Gardiner of East Hoathly, and the wind was in the right direction to take the balloon over his house.

Henry Green was the brother of professional balloonist Charles Green. He embarked on a ballooning career when he found that the gas produced at the end of the distillation process, by the gas companies that were being set up all over the country, was ideal for inflating balloons. He was able to persuade many of companies to put it into separate holders and negotiated a discount price for the gas in return for publicising, by his balloon flights, this new fuel for lighting and heating.

This naive illustration formed part of Henry Green's announcement in the **Sussex Weekly Advertiser** *of his intention of making 'an ASCENT with his MAGNIFICENT balloon on Monday, the 22nd of September, 1828, at Three o'clock precisely'.*

Parish does not want a police force

1830-38

The Cliffe is administered by the manor of Ringmer, the lordship of which is held by the Duke of Dorset, and a Constable and Headborough are appointed annually at the court leet held at the Bear Hotel.

Thomas Woollgar, in recording information 'from an old manuscript' in the second volume of his *Spicelegia*, expressed surprise that manorial authority still pertained in the Cliffe where:

> out of one hundred and twelve houses there is but one Copyhold, all the rest being Freehold and the whole Vill or parish with the Fair Place, Lands, Yards, Warfs and premises contains no more than Thirty Six acres of Land.

The inhabitants appear to be quite content to leave the keeping of law and order in the hands of the officers appointed by the manor court. When the Commissioners for Improving the Vill and Parish of the Cliffe – a body roughly equivalent to a present-day parish council which was set up under the Cliffe Improvement Act – met on 3 September to consider setting up a police force the proposal was thrown out by nine votes to six. The parish is used to keeping its own peace. It formed its own night patrols in the autumn of 1830 when, throughout the south, unemployed farm labourers and those still in work but on starvation wages, began burning ricks, barns and crops to draw attention to their plight.

The vestry's annual meetings, at which the Commissioners are elected, are not now confined to the Bear Hotel and the Dorset Arms but held in turn at 'all the inns in the parish with room for them'.

VOCATIONAL TRAINING

6 May 1823

The overseers of poor today brought before the justices 'a poor child, aged 12, Moses Philcox', to be apprenticed to South Street blacksmith, Samuel Leney, because his mother, Lucy Philcox, is not able to maintain him.

The boy has to live with and serve his master 'in all lawful Business according to his Power, Wit and Ability, and honestly, orderly and obediently in all Things, demean and behave himself' until he reaches the age of twenty-one.

In return he is to be instructed in 'the art and mystery of a blacksmith and be provided with Meat, Drink, Apparel, Lodging, Washing and all other things necessary and fit for an Apprentice.'

Leney was to be paid a total of £20 by the parish for training Moses.

REFORM ACT GIVES £10-A-YEAR TENANTS A VOTE

4 July 1832

The Reform Act has extended the vote from the landed interest to adult male householders paying an annual rent of £10 and Southover and the Cliffe have combined with Lewes to enfranchise their eligible residents. The Act has also done away with fifty-six rotten and pocket boroughs, and thirty boroughs with less than 4,000 inhabitants have each lost one member. Today the passing of the Act was celebrated with a dinner for 600 people in Mrs Gaston's orchard in Malling Street. The first to be elected under the new system, which has increased the electorate from 700 to 877, were Thomas Read Kemp and Sir Charles Richard Blunt of Heathfield Park.

Charles Wille – timber merchant, diarist, Constable of the Hundred . . .

From 1832

Cliffe has had, throughout the centuries, merchants and traders prepared to devote time and energy to the well-being of their fellow citizens as well as to their own commercial interests. Such a one is timber merchant Charles Wille, the site of whose sawpit between Nos 57 and 79 in South Street is now occupied by Wille (often mis-spelt Willie) Cottages, a terrace of six Victorian houses to which a seventh was added in the early 1980s.

From 1832, until his death at the age of eighty-one in 1878, Charles Wille kept a diary. In it he noted the journeys he made, meetings he attended, accidents that occurred to people and property, results of elections, the book he was reading on a walk in Eastbourne – it was one of Edward Gibbon's five volume *History of the Decline and Fall of the Roman Empire* – and almost everything in the way of the weather.

The extracts from the diaries, published in the October and November issues of the 1929 *Sussex County Magazine* reveal little about the man. Was he a Whig or a Tory? A Dissenter or Church of England? Such entries as this one for 24 December 1832:

> Sussex Election clos'd. Cavendish and Curteis returned, fine morning and afternoon.

says more about the weather than the writer's politics. An entry on 29 November 1850 is equally nonpartisan about religion:

> Town Meetg. on acct. of papal Aggression. Dissenters and Church met on Platform.

Charles Wille was thirty three when he 'sat for my likeness' to portrait painter Archibald Archer.

Young Charles spent four years in Guildford, where he was apprenticed to an ironmonger. He changed trades on his return to Lewes, joined the family firm and settled down to work. And work he did, as the diaries show. A typical day was 4 January 1833 when he:

> Rose ¼ after 4 – went into the Counting house, wrote till near 8. Served on the Grand Jury the remainder of the day, returned home ½ Pt.10 in the Evening.

In 1836, when he was thirty nine, he was chosen to be Headborough of the Hundred of Ringmer and in that capacity, on 11 January 1837, he:

> In the evening went to all the Beer shops and Public houses.

He was later a Constable of the Hundred, a Commissioner for the Vill of the Cliffe, and made frequent visits to the workhouse in South Street as a member, and for two years vice chairman, of the Board of Guardians of the Lewes Union. He was also a great traveller, sometimes in the way of business visiting customers in Kent and Sussex and timber importers as far afield as Yorkshire, by horse and carriage. He often went to London by stage coach to see the sights:

> 1851 May 16th. Went to the top of St. Paul's, then to Greenwich, & in the Evening to Surry Gardens
> May 30th. Fine day. Went to Exhibition.

The moment the trains came he was either on them or writing about them:

1846 April 6th. The Engine ran on the line from Southram to Kingstone for the 1st time.

July 3rd – Fine day. Went to Westham & Hastings & back by rail.

On 1 October the following year the Keymer line opened and he:

Went to London & back. Went by Lewes train to 3 Bridges – back by Brighton . . .

In 1853, when he was fifty-six, Charles Wille retired, noting in his diary, 'August 13th Fine day. Clos'd Business', and set about visiting places of interest in the Sussex countryside. He would cover a fair distance in a day, by various means of transport. On 27 June 1855 he:

Went to Hastings. Visited Old Humphrey's grave. Went to Battle by rail – on to Robertsbridge by a Gig – to Etchingham by Rail & to Burwash afoot.

The following year he moved to Newick and noted on 5 November that 'the evening was kept up lively' in that village. The diaries from 1860 to 1865 are missing. Wille may have left them in London where he was living from 1864, but his reasons for being there he does not disclose. The only reference to his sojourn in the capital is this brief entry in the 1866 diary:

March 31st. Overcast, with showers. Left London for Lewes – just 2 years absence.

The later diaries have more references to items of national than of local interest, indicating that the writer was spending more time at home with the daily newspapers than getting out and about. Home was once again Ryder's Well, a villa on the edge of Ringmer Park into which Charles had moved with his new bride. When he joined his father in the timber business he had moved with his young family into the firm's house in the yard at South Street and leased Ryder's Well to the grandparents of William Grantham KC who, when not in court, spent his time encouraging the youth of Sussex to play stoolball.

The last entries are for 1876:

May 29th. Balloon from Crystal Palace ascended from old Timber wharf.

November 6th. Fine, Eveng clear. The demonstration (for the 5th) very good.

December 6th. Very fine day (heavy floods) . . .

Wille's trade card shows the woods he sold and from where they were imported.

WILLE ON THE WEATHER

On **29 November 1836**, the winter of the avalanche, Charles Wille recorded : 'A Storm of Wind abt. 11 in the forenoon' which blew down several barns, uprooted trees, damaged windmills and the Chain Pier in Brighton where several lives were lost'.

1839

'June 18th. Hot day. Thunderstorm at night kill'd 93 Lambs & Sheep at South Ease & 1 horse.'

1846

'February 28th. Very fine day. Like a May day. This month now closed has been a warm open month such as I never before knew.'

1848

'November 17th. Aurora very peculiar in the Evening – the whole of the atmosphere Red like fire.'

1852

'October 5th. A very great flood from the rain of the preceding day – larger than known since 1814, coming very near the High St. of Cliffe (neap tides). October 27th. Damp day. A greater flood than the last, flowing [into] the Bear Inn and Malling Street.'

1858

'October 5th. Fine day. The Comet pass'd by a Star appearing about a foot below the Star – the Star keeping about the same distance and setting together abt. 9 0'clock.'

Eight lives lost in South Street avalanche

1836

In the *Guinness Book of Records*, under the heading: WORST DISASTERS IN THE UK, is the entry:

Avalanche 8 lives lost
Lewes, East Sussex
27 December 1836

It had started snowing heavily on Christmas night and on Monday 26 December the wind blew hard all day from the north east and drifted the snow into a continuous ridge 10-15ft thick along the brow of the cliffs above South Street. The scene was described in the *Sussex Weekly Advertiser* of 5 January:

Tons and tons of it seemed to hang in a delicately turned wreath as lightsome as a feather but which, in fact, bowed down by its own weight, threatened destruction to everything beneath

There were fears for the safety of the people living in the South Malling workhouse cottages that formed Boulders Row and these became more acute on the Monday evening when a fall of snow from the clifftop on to Charles Wille's timberyard destroyed a sawing shed, forcing it from its position upwards of 40ft. Wille warned the cottagers to move but they would not do so.

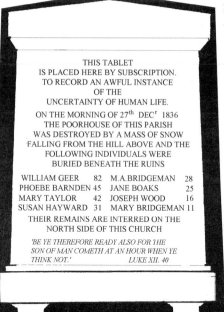

THIS TABLET
IS PLACED HERE BY SUBSCRIPTION.
TO RECORD AN AWFUL INSTANCE OF THE
UNCERTAINTY OF HUMAN LIFE.
ON THE MORNING OF 27th DEC^r 1836
THE POORHOUSE OF THIS PARISH
WAS DESTROYED BY A MASS OF SNOW
FALLING FROM THE HILL ABOVE AND THE
FOLLOWING INDIVIDUALS WERE
BURIED BENEATH THE RUINS

WILLIAM GEER	82	M.A.BRIDGEMAN	28
PHOEBE BARNDEN	45	JANE BOAKS	25
MARY TAYLOR	42	JOSEPH WOOD	16
SUSAN HAYWARD	31	MARY BRIDGEMAN	11

THEIR REMAINS ARE INTERRED ON THE
NORTH SIDE OF THIS CHURCH

'BE YE THEREFORE READY ALSO FOR THE SON OF MAN COMETH AT AN HOUR WHEN YE THINK NOT.' LUKE XII. 40

Next morning the snow that hung over South Street was intersected by fissures and the danger was even more evident. Again the cottagers were warned and a few of them moved out, but others, although places of refuge were offered them, decided to stay.

At about 10am on the Tuesday Robert Higham, licensee of the Schooner Inn, climbed up under the snow to assess the extent of the danger. What he saw there prompted him to rush into Boulders Row and beg the inmates to move for their lives. He had just got clear of the cottages when a huge field of solid snow slid down the steep slope with tremendous force and smashed into and buried the seven end houses. The newspaper takes up the story:

The mass appeared to strike houses at the base, heave them upwards and then break over like a gigantic wave to dash them bodily into the road . . . The scene which ensued was heart-rending. Children were screaming for their parents and women were rushing through the street with frantic gestures in search of their offspring; while in the middle of the consternation men were hastening from all quarters with spades and shovels for the purposes of extricating the sufferers . . .

This oil painting of the avalanche by Thomas Henwood is on display in Anne of Cleves House museum.
Photo: Sussex Archaeological Society

AN EARLY WARNING OF GLOBAL WARMING

Concern about climate change and global warming is not new. William Thomson of School Hill, Lewes, preceded his account of the avalanche, published by his daughter after his death, with this observation:

'There is little doubt that the climate of England is not so severe as formerly; the snow neither falls so deeply, nor does it continue to lie so long on the ground. Whether this may be in part or wholly attributed to cultivation and drainage may admit of argument, but the fact of our generally having mild winters is indisputable.'

The weather in the last six months of 1836 did not support that statement. The coldest summer day ever recorded was on 20 July when it was a chilly 52°F (10°C) and there were great gales in November.

'The whole of the ancient and splendid elms before the Deanery at Malling were blown down by one tremendous blast from, I think, the ENE, and they laid there for some years,' wrote Mr C R Smith of Portslade in a letter to the editor of the *Sussex Daily News.*

There was an inquest on Wednesday on the eight victims of the avalanche and evidence was given to the effect that the cottages, in which forty people lived, were 'as firmly built as that description of houses generally are'. One of the occupants, James Rook, said that he saw the snow fall. He had the moment before spoken to Mrs Taylor in the street and begged her not to go towards the cottages. Her death left eleven children motherless.

The jury returned a verdict of accidental death, and all those who died, with the exception of thirty-four-year-old Susan Haywood, who presumably was not Church of England, were buried in one grave in the churchyard of St Michael's, South Malling. The route to the church was still deep in snow, which had to be cleared to allow the waggons bearing the coffins of the victims, their forty relatives, friends and followers, to get through. 'It was indeed a heap of sorrow and grief to spectators', wrote Charles Wille in his diary on 30 December.

A committee under the chairmanship of William Thomson was appointed to raise funds to compensate the helpers and the victims' families. Nearly £400 was deposited at Lewes Bank out of which £91 2s 0d went to 'labour at the ruins'; £35 3s 6d was spent on 'printing, hire of tools, stationery, hire of brooms, constables and other incidental expenses'; £193 went to the families of the victims and £75 was deposited in the Savings Bank for the eight orphaned or injured children.

A boy recalls his days at a dame school

When the daughter of music master and teacher of dancing, Edwin George Peckham, died as a result of a virulent attack of smallpox the undertakers refused to go into her parents' house to remove the body for burial. Eventually two old men from the House of Industry, who had both been vaccinated against the disease in 1774, volunteered to do what was necessary and for this service they each were given half a crown. The girl was put in her coffin just as she lay and when the men returned to Union Place their clothes were burned on a fire that had been specially prepared in the workhouse yard.

The smallpox victim was buried at midnight in the parish burial ground in Malling Street.

'It was reported to be by torchlight but I believe three or four lanterns were used at the graveside,' writes James Morris. 'The tolling of the church bell at night caused some consternation among the inhabitants, and, although living but five houses away, I was afraid even to look out of the window.'

When she was widowed in 1826 at the age of fifty-one Elizabeth Page opened a school 'for a select number of young ladies' in South Street. She called it the Delap Hall Seminary after the poet, playwright and rector of Iford, Dr John Delap, who lived there until his death in 1812.

Among the young ladies were some even younger gentlemen. James Morris, son of Cliffe iron founder Ebenezer Morris, was one of them. 'I was four or five and dressed in petticoats for it was customary for both sexes to be dressed alike', he writes in one of a series of articles about the Cliffe published in the *Eastbourne Courier* in the 1880s. When he was put in boys' clothes he wore yellow nankeen trousers, a blue cashmere coat with lapels reaching to the knees, a large white collar with a frill round the edge and a white horsehair cap with a blue tassel.

'There were about thirty scholars of both sexes, about a third being boys. The writing and the arithmetic was done on slates. In the afternoon the girls did plain needlework, the older boys taking turns in reading stories or history for the edification of the others,' he recalls.

'The punishments consisted of the stocks, of which there were half-a-dozen. These were made of wood and about eighteen inches long and nine inches wide. On the top were nailed some pieces of wood at right angles into which the feet were placed. There were also backboards, which are too well known to need description. The slipper was also occasionally in requisition, both sexes coming in for a fair share'.

A child was walking with a serving maid along North Street, Cliffe, when a bullock rushed at her and tossed her clean through the window of George Hoey's china shop. She lay there, surrounded by broken glass and china, but although she was considerably cut around the head and face she was not seriously hurt. The bullock's owner, butcher Thomas King, had to pay £27 for repairs to the premises.

James Morris saw the window shortly after the accident. He thought it was a wonder that the girl had not been killed on the spot.

Coronation is celebrated with a hot dinner for 600

2 July 1838

The inhabitants of the Cliffe turned down an invitation to celebrate the coronation of Queen Victoria with the borough of Lewes and its neighbouring parishes. Instead they decided to confine the treat to their own parish and a subscription was raised for the purpose of providing a hot dinner for 600 poor people.

And what a dinner it was. It took four waggons to bring the 468lbs of prime joints of beef, mutton, pork and veal and eighty-six plum puddings, each weighing 4½lbs and 'a proportionate amount of beer' to the two 225ft-long tables set out in Malling Field, loaned for the occasion by pork butcher, Samuel Relf.

At 12 noon, to the sound of the pealing of the church bells and the roar of cannon firing salutes from barges moored on the river, the poor, 'in happy procession headed by the constables, headborough, churchwardens and children waving flags', made their way through the streets of the town to their seats at the tables.

'After it was over rural sports were the order of the day and about 150 ladies and gentlemen and the principal inhabitants of the parish sat down to a repast in a booth – Mr Farnes presiding', reported the *East Sussex News* in a retrospective account of the coronation, published in 1887 for Queen Victoria's golden jubilee.

No more uphill walks to the post

1838

Cliffe residents and traders have no longer to climb School Hill to post their letters at the Lewes Receiving House at 44 High Street. A sub-office to receive letters for onward despatch has been opened at 51 Cliffe High Street and there are daily collections from it at 10am and 7pm on weekdays and at 10am only on Sundays.

Street pillar boxes and wall-mounted letter boxes were introduced in 1855 and a year later Daniel Morris's shop in Malling Street became another sub office.

ACT PENALISES THE POOR
1834

The Poor Law Amendment Act of 1834 has combined groups of parishes into Unions to save money and ruled that all able-bodied paupers in need of help have to be admitted to a workhouse to receive it. The parishes of the Cliffe and South Malling are now in the Lewes Union with Ringmer and Southover.

Existing workhouses, including the House of Industry in South Street have been taken over and will be administered by a Board of Guardians. They are to be run on the strictest lines to deter the poor from going on the parish. In spite of protests from all over the country, the Act is not being altered. Locally, however, its more inhuman clauses are being ignored.

'PECULIAR' CHANGE
1846

The church of St Thomas in the Cliffe, held by the dean and canons of the College of St Michael the Archangel, Malling from 1349, and as a 'peculiar' of the Archbishops of Canterbury from 1574, has been transferred to the Crown. It now comes under the jurisdiction of the diocese of Chichester.

The arrival of the railway

1839-1893

The first intimation the inhabitants of Cliffe and South Malling had of a new form of public transport coming to the area was an increase of traffic on the Ouse. Construction material for the 1,475ft long 96ft high viaduct being built at Balcombe to carry the Brighton railway line over the river was daily brought up by barge. The railway company paid the river authority a toll of a halfpenny a ton per mile for chalk, lime, manure, corn and road materials. By June 1846 the London, Brighton and South Coast Railway had a double track line to the station it had built in Friars Walk and from there a single track line was laid, in a mere eight weeks, to Hastings. The railway did not cross into the Cliffe and South Malling until 1868 when the line from Lewes to Uckfield was opened. It ran from the first station – in Friars Walk – across an iron girder bridge near Every's Phoenix Iron works onto a causeway across Malling Brooks and joined the Lewes to Keymer junction line at Hamsey.

A tug tows a brig through the bridge that replaced the lift and roll type when the line was electrified in 1935.

Southerham's first railway bridge was built at the junction of lines to Polegate via Glynde and Berwick and the new line to Newhaven via Southease and Rodmell Halt. It was made of wood, with a 31ft long centre section that could be drawn back over the north west bank to allow ships to pass through. This wooden bridge was replaced in 1893 by one built of iron. It had five spans, each made of four iron girders, and it needed a gang of thirty men to operate the lift and roll back opening system. They did not have to do it too often. The number of sea-going vessels with fixed masts using the river declined rapidly when the railway offered to carry coal, clay, timber and other heavy freight without charge between the port of Newhaven and Lewes.

The railway had its teething troubles. Timber merchant Charles Wille noted in his diary on 10 September 1846 that the 'luggage train from Hastings ran down an incline to the brook, went over the bank and the engine fell into the Spring Ditch. No lives lost'. Wille had a grandstand view of the incident as he lived at his yard and wharf on the Cliffe bank of the Ouse in South Street, just opposite the Spring Ditch. Two days later he recorded:

Fine day. The Engine, after much labour, got out of the ditch without harm to any.

Cliffe's open sewers are now closed

1849

The five open culverts that carry flood water from Malling Brooks, through drains beneath Cliffe High Street to the river where it bends to the east towards Southerham, have been covered over. The Commission of Sewers, empowered by the Cliffe Improvement Act of 1828 to levy a tax on the inhabitants to pay for the work, has paved over the insanitary open water courses. They now provide such useful access passageways at right angles to the main street as North Court, English Passage and Foundry Lane. Anyone emptying 'offal or filth' into the new 18-inch diameter drains is liable to a fine of £5.

The system of culverts is possibly of monastic origin. Both the secular canons of the College of St Michael the Archangel at Malling and the Cluniacs at the Priory of St Pancras, sited as they were by the river, would have had a vested interest in flood prevention. And it is significant that Robert Croham, prior of St Pancras, went, 'at his own cost and charge', accompanied by Sir Edward Bray, to Flanders 'to view and see things there whereby they might learn experience' and brought back with them 'the wisest men and of the most experience they could hire'.

The Commission of Sewers for the county of Sussex, set up by Henry VIII in 1534 to see to the repairing of sea walls and the 'cleansing of rivers, public streams, ditches and other conduits whereby any waters are carried off', did a considerable amount of

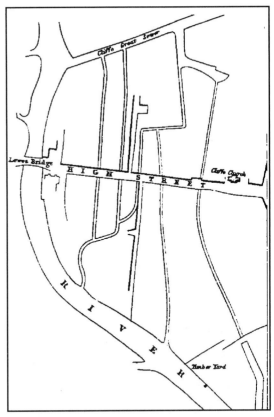

The 'ancient sewers intersecting the Cliffe' from a map drawn in 1842 by John Woollgar, clerk to the Cliffe Commissioners.

remedial work on the 2,500 acres of the Lewes Levels. It then had problems recovering the money it had spent. Sir John Gage, in a letter from 'my power house at Firle' to the Lord Privy Seal, Thomas Cromwell, complained of landowners refusing to pay the water tax of sixteen shillings an acre levied on them and sought his advice and support.

Cliffe householders had equally little regard for health, hygiene and the common good. They used the five open culverts as convenient depositories for every kind of waste and would often refuse to pay for the deepening and clearing of the ones for which they were responsible unless brought before the Watercourt and fined for not doing so.

ACCIDENT AT SITE OF THE 'SNOWDROP'
21 April 1844

Four years after the South Street avalanche an inn was built near the site and named the Snowdrop.

Last week there was another accident there but fortunately not a fatal one. Carpenter Henry Gorringe broke a leg 'and was very much hurt' when he fell from the back roof of the inn's stables, where he had been working.

GRAVEYARD ENLARGED
1846

The parish burial ground on the east side of Malling Street, last enlarged in 1796 after an outbreak of smallpox, is to be extended by a further 3,340 sq ft.

The addition crosses the parish boundary, 88ft of its frontage to Malling Street being in the Cliffe and the remaining 18ft in South Malling.

NEW SCHOOL
1848

St Michael the Archangel church has opened a school for up to 100 pupils in Malling Street, almost opposite the Coombe. Miss Emma Wood is its first headmistress.

Bonfires are back on the streets

1850s

The re-establishment of the Roman Catholic hierarchy in England by Pope Pius IX brought fires, torches, tar barrels, rockets and rousers back on to the streets of Lewes after several years of off-road celebrations at Wallands.

There was a huge fire at Cliffe Corner on the Fifth and another outside County Hall, where a 3,000 strong crowd listened approvingly to a denunciation of papal interference in the religious affairs of the country. Bonfire had become respectable and as the years passed the pageantry of protest became much more organised.

By 1853 the Cliffe Bonfire Society was in existence. The costume of disguise for its members was a white shirt worn outside red trousers. The Borough society, which was formed at about the same time, wore white trousers and black and white striped jerseys.

A tar barrel that survived some of the early runs is now on display at Anne of Cleves House.

The evening started with a tar barrel run up the High Street to Cliffe bridge and back to the fire site at Cliffe Corner where, after they had been paraded through the streets, the various effigies and tableaux were burned. As the years passed and more societies were formed, the parades of costumed figures carrying lighted torches and accompanied by 'bands of music' became more organised and formed a larger part of the evening's entertainment for the onlookers.

It was the Cliffe Bonfire Society that introduced a 'Lord Bishop in full canonicals' to preach a sermon before the burning of the effigies. 'Thou shalt not steal' would have been an apt text for the sermon at the Cliffe's 1859 fire for on it was an effigy of the member who had made off with the society's money box. It was burnt with far more enthusiasm than the effigy of the Pope.

Mary Hannah's memorial to her horse

The initials MHR on the boundary stone outside Wayside on Malling Hill are those of Mary Hannah Rickman (1835-1905), sister of Quaker merchant Richard Peters Rickman.

Horses were the love of Mary Hannah's life. She was a good and most considerate rider, always sitting forward and insisting on a saddle with a single pommel to avoid giving any horse she rode a sore back. But she did rather go to extremes – wearing one brown stocking and one white one when riding one of her mounts so that her legs matched the colour markings of its legs.

She filled the meadow beside her house in Spences Field with horses that had been ill-treated or were too old to work – of which there was a plentiful supply. Often drivers, wishing to get rid of an old nag for cash, would chastise it outside her gates on which was a notice reading:

> UPHILL WHIP ME NOT;
> DOWNHILL HURRY ME NOT.

and Miss Rickman could be relied upon to rush out, purse in hand, and buy the animal. When her favourite riding horse, Charlie, dropped dead on Malling Hill on his way to the Downs for exercise, Mary Hannah, who always got up at 4am amd went to bed at 4pm, had him:

> . . . laid to rest in the first hour of 3 April in a still air, just touched with frost, under the clear light of the moon and stars . . .

Above the grave she had a gigantic mound erected. It had a concrete core and a seat at the top approached by a winding path bordered by a low hedge. In a published appreciation of Charlie she says:

> It is consoling to reflect that, up to the last, he felt perfect confidence in the kindness and goodwill of all who had to do with him; that, up to the last, *he knew that he was loved.* Would that every horse, that all cattle and every domesticated creature, could feel and know as much . . .

Mary Hannah's interest in the animal kingdom was reflected in the decorations in her dining room. The stuffed head of a tiger, flanked by imitation grasses, glared out, behind glass, from a hole in the wall. She had bought it at an auction sale and had hoped to get the lion's head that was also on offer but someone else outbid her.

It was in these exotic surroundings that she gave an annual Twelfth Night every year for all the Quaker children in the area.

All the news from 'Cliffe, Lewes, Old England'

1853

News of the 'wonderful floods', the price of crops and coal, the preparedness of the local militia, the bonfire celebrations, who has died and who has emigrated is included by Samuel Elphick in his letter of 17 November to his brother, Richard, who had emigrated with his wife and family to Australia to dig for gold.

After reassuring Richard that his father and mother, brothers and sisters are all well 'except for Joseph, a grocer and draper by trade, who was burnt on the Fifth of November by a fire ball at Battle' and 'are not married any of us yet' he goes on:

We have had such a wonderful flood in Lewes a twelvemonth back. We went, four of us, in the soap house boat into the hay barn and we had two floods in about three weeks. The last one was the highest by several inches and came up the lane by the soap house door. The lower rooms at the Bear near the bridge were flooded and our gardens were nearly covered and the cellar nearly full. Weeks of almost continuous rainfall caused serious flooding in Malling Street and the lower parts of the Cliffe.

After listing the price per quarter of wheat, oats, peas and beans and grumbling about farming 'being a very poor trade for some time past' Samuel gives his brother 'a little account of Lewes and the neighbourhood':

Our old Castle warehouse is pulled down making a nice open yard or lawn and there is a fine large new Gaol built just on the Brighton road close to Smarts Mills. They are now making a place for drilling the Artillery Company of the Sussex Militia. I should tell you, though, that the Government have called out the Militia to the extent of some thousands and intend increasing them still more.

He then names 'several people gone from Lewes to Australia', among them:

Mr Beyer, an exciseman's son; Mr Harvey, spirit merchant son; Mr Tanner, watchmaker's son; Mr Cheele from Southover; two Mr Valentines from Chailey.

And he adds:

Mr and Mrs Weller next door to us are both dead, Mr Hazelden still works at Mr Berry's but he is moved somewhere round to near Waterloo Street. Master Cane, the park carter, is dead. Dr Colgate of East Hoathly is dead. Abram Funnell has left and set up in South Street where Rickman and Kenner's old premises are and sells just the same sort of goods we do and tries to get all our trade he can. Isaac is living in Malling Street and keeps a meal and flour shop and is getting on pretty well I think; he has three children and Abram has got three children. Old Mrs Funnell is living and is middling, except for the rheumatics.

Bonfire, he says, is 'stronger than ever':

We had in the Cliffe about 23 tar barrels and a first rate German band from Brighton and flags, torches and guernseys and white ducks, such a jolly go in and no opposition. Old Bacon the printer don't like it much and sent out in his paper [*The Sussex Agricultural Express*] a lot of abuse and lies about it, so the boys sent him a parcel of potato pearings and cabbage leaves for his hog and they also carry a picture of a large hog on a flag and call it Peter's Ghost on bonfire night.

He signs his letter:

I am, yours sincerely,
Saml. Elphick.
Cliffe, Lewes, Old England

Volunteer fire brigade is formed

1864-65

The Cliffe has formed its own volunteer fire brigade. It is captained by builder Benjamin Thorpe, and consists of a lieutenant, an engineer and seventeen firemen, all of whom live locally.

There was a ready response to an appeal for funds to buy a fire engine and a Paxton appliance, exactly like one supplied by the firm of Merryweather to the Prince of Wales for use at Sandringham, was selected. It cost £120, less than half the £270 raised, but there were still hoses and buckets to be paid for as well as helmets and uniforms for the crew.

The engine arrived by rail from London on 30 June and on 6 July, reported the *East Sussex News*: '. . . drawn by four spanking greys, and accompanied by twenty members of the brigade and Captain Thorpe in uniform and ready for action' it was paraded from Lewes station to Winterbourne Hollow and then down the High Street to the Cliffe. The pumping capacity of the appliance was tested at the waterworks mains at Cliffe Corner and there was a private fire-fighting demonstration in the evening before it was moved into the engine house built for it in the Fair Place. The 'beautiful new engine' was badly damaged at one of the first fires to which it was taken. One of the walls of Broad's candle factory in Market Street collapsed almost on top of it and the appliance was 'unable to render any further assistance'.

Any suggestion of rivalry between the Lewes and Cliffe brigades was firmly denied by their captains but in January 1866 the Cliffe's secretary, James Frank, wrote a rather pained letter to *East Sussex News* explaining that they were late at Allchorn's Farm fire because they did not know about it until they saw the town engine go past.

'We have a first class engine recently purchased by subscriptions from the inhabitants and neighbouring gentry,' he said. 'All we ask is to be immediately informed of a fire.'

William Bradford's design for John Harvey's Bridge Wharf brewery, from the **Brewers' Journal** *of 1831*

Four breweries are in business

1860s

There are currently four breweries in the Cliffe and South Malling. They are, in age order, Monk's Bear Yard Brewery, Harvey's Bridge Wharf Brewery, South Malling Steam Brewery, and Hillman's Southdown Brewery.

Teetotal Quaker John Rickman, who inherited the brewery started in Bear Yard in the eighteenth century by his grandfather, Thomas Rickman, sold it in 1817 to Thomas Wood and his partner, Thomas Tamplin, younger brother of Richard, founder of the Tamplin empire.

John Harvey, who had set up as a wine and spirit merchant in Cliffe High Street in 1790, brewed by arrangement in Bear Yard until 1838 when Wood died and his brewery was bought by Edwin Monk and Sons.

At about the same time John Harvey bought Bridge Wharf for £3,707, so connecting his premises to the river and providing himself with water-borne access for fuel and grain. On the site were three houses, two coal yards, a timber yard and two covered warehouses. New premises, designed by William Bradford, were completed in 1881 and incorporated in the decorative ironwork on top of the malthouse was the 1620 weathervane from Cliffe church. It had been sold for 4s 2d with the

The counting house of the Southdown brewery in Thomas Street

The South Malling Steam brewery, rebuilt after the disastrous fire of 1866, is on the left of Malling Street, coming from the north.

market bell and other scrap metal by the churchwardens in 1751 and was not seen again until 1880 when it was unearthed during excavations near the church and given to a member of the Harvey family.

Southdown Brewery was established in Thomas Street in 1838 by Alfred Hillman. Apart from a fatal accident there on 4 February 1863 when William Gresham-Wiles fell into a brew tun, it traded peaceably with its ten licensed outlets until 1895 when it was bought by Augustus and Thomas Manning. They had great plans for expansion and three years later had acquired a brewery in East Grinstead, another in Cuckfield, had picked up Monk's Bear Yard brewery, bought ninety-three pubs and were listed on the Stock Exchange.

South Malling Brewery, built in 1821 by Alexander Elmsley, was burnt down on 14 June 1866 and had to be rebuilt. The newly-formed Cliffe Volunteer Fire Brigade had been quickly on the scene and the Lewes appliance had also been hauled to the blaze but they could not get the fire under control because of a shortage of water.

Elmsley installed a steam brewing plant in the imposing new premises he built after this fire and traded from there as a wine, spirit and cider merchant, brewer, maltster, and agent for Allsopp's and Bass's pale ales and Guinness's stout until his death in 1875. The brewery was acquired by Bishop and Son in 1898 and sold at auction, with its remaining two pubs, to Tamplins a year later.

STAGE HAND IS FOUND DEAD IN BED

13 January 1865

The Ewers Pavilion Theatre, which has spent the past sixteen years touring through Surrey and West Sussex, set up its marquee in South Street, Cliffe a week ago.

Today one of the stage hands, who was lodging at the Thatched House Inn, was found dead in bed when he was called for his dinner at 12.30pm. Richard Burton, a former soldier who was present at the siege of Sebastopol, had recently been discharged from Brighton hospital as incurable.

The last cries of the last town crier

HARRIET'S IS A DISORDERLY HOUSE

21 April 1865

Edward Evans, licensee of the Bargeman's Arms in South Street, has been committed for trial at the next quarter sessions for keeping a disorderly house.

The complainants are two Cliffe Commissioners, Edward Hillman and John Wilmhurst. They told the magistrates that Evans' beershop, locally known as 'Harriet's' was a house of ill fame and it was frequented by men and women of loose character.

GIRLS TRAINED TO SERVE

1 August 1867

Lewes Girls' Training School has opened at Delap Hall, South Street – premises formerly occupied by the late Elizabeth Page's Seminary for Young Ladies.

It offers an elementary education to children from 10-15 years of age and prepares them for domestic service. The school, which declares that it is entirely unsectarian in its views, is run by a 'committee of ladies' and has two Quakers, Sylvia Rickman and Frances Trusted, as secretary and treasurer respectively.

8 December 1865

Thomas Gibb, a forty-six-year-old clockmaker of 6 North Street, Cliffe, was chosen today, at a Court Leet for the Hundred of Ringmer held at the Bear Hotel, to succeed the late John Mabbott as town crier. His predecessor, who died two months ago, aged between eighty and ninety, had been employed at the Verralls' soap factory at Southerham and then at the gas works when these were opened in 1822. When he became too old and frail to work he was retired on a company pension.

Among the Cliffe crier's regular announcements was the arrival of fresh fish from Newhaven. It was brought up river by barge, which moored at the town wharf on the Lewes side of the bridge. Its arrival was announced with the traditional cry of:

Oyez! Oyez! Oyez!
Just arrived and now selling at the bridge, Lewes
Fine fresh scallops, twopence a dozen
Full roed mackerel, sixteen a shilling.

Thomas Gibb was the parish's last crier and his last cries were concerned with the various requirements of the Municipal Corporations (New Charters) Act of 1877, which was to bring the Cliffe's independence to an end.

There was an average of ninety-two pupils on the register of South Malling Parochial School but where were they all when this picture was taken in the 1880s? Photo: Sussex Archaeological Society.

Malling church has a £600 facelift

1873

There was little that the Victorians enjoyed more than refurbishing churches. Regrettably, their enthusiasm for the task all too often resulted in the loss of items of great historical interest. Any medieval wall paintings that had survived the zeal of Puritan purges of the Commonwealth were likely to be covered with whitewash; old pulpits replaced; and choir stalls discarded – carved misericords and all.

Fortunately the work to be carried out on the Church of St Michael the Archangel at South Malling is of a constructive rather than of a destructive nature. A new chancel

The interior of the church before the restoration work started. From a pencil sketch by Esme Currey of Malling Deanery.

window is to be installed and filled with stained glass as a memorial to the late Reverend William Courthope, curate of St Michael's for seven years from 1842. It is the gift of his brother, George Campion Courthope of Malling Deanery, who is patron of the living.

By taking down the screen and gallery at the west end space will be provided in the tower for a schoolroom. An organ chamber and a vestry are to be added on the north side, the pews and pulpit replaced and the roof and other parts of the church repaired. A form of warming apparatus is to be installed and a new reading desk. The total cost of the work is expected to be about £600 and the church will be closed for some weeks while it is being done.

BREAK-IN AT POST OFFICE
19 November 1877

A thief or thieves broke into the sub-post office at 15 Cliffe High Street while the postmistress, Sarah Cripps, and her mother were at church and stole cash, cheques and stamps to the value of some £45.

The premises had been securely locked when they left at 6.30pm but when they returned at 9.30pm after visiting relatives, they found the front door open and the shop in disarray. A cash box containing £15 in notes, a £15 cheque, £11 10s in gold and about £2 in silver and copper was missing and about 27s worth of loose postage and receipt stamps.

CHAPEL IS DEMOLISHED
1879

The chapel which gave Chapel Hill its name has been demolished and three cottages and a workshop built on the site.

When founded in 1775 by the Countess of Huntington it was the first dissenting chapel in the Cliffe. However, doctrinal differences caused ministers to depart to other congregations. It is to these congregations that the proceeds from the sale of the chapel have passed.

Typhoid epidemic: Town water supply was contaminated

27 November 1874

In the past four months there have been 435 cases of typhoid fever in the Lewes area and twenty-seven people have died from the disease. The outbreak started with seven cases in the week ending 1 August and in the next fortnight there were forty more. The epidemic continued until early September when there was a decline in the number of people affected. However, this was only a brief respite for there were a further 197 cases up to 24 October.

These facts and figures prefaced the report given to Lewes Borough Council by Dr Thorne, an inspector from the medical department of the Local Government Board brought in to inquire into the outbreak and its cause or causes. His conclusion, delivered to a meeting attended by, among others, Cliffe iron founder, Ebenezer Morris, chairman of the Lewes Waterworks Company, was that the town water supply was to blame.

The source of the infection had not been easy to trace. Typhoid, or enteric, fever, was associated with the pollution of air and water by human excrement and the disease had appeared suddenly in all parts of the town – in Southover, which was in another watershed and Cliffe, which was separated from Lewes by the river and had a different system of drainage.

Forty-five cases, involving forty-three houses, were investigated. Twelve of them had no cisterns – they received a direct supply to their water closets, so air contaminated by infected excrement could be drawn from the pans into the main sewers. The Ouse received all the sewage from the town at low water and Professor du Pré, who had analysed samples of the water, said that in his opinion accidental pollution of the supply had occurred when tidal water had flowed into the inlet of the waterworks. A dam had since been put up to prevent any recurrence and a general system of disinfecting the mains had been organised by the sanitary authorities. The sewers were now also periodically flushed and disinfected.

'Science has triumphed, the evil has been remedied . . .' commented the *East Sussex News,* which printed the report in full.

NO FIRES OR FIREWORKS ON THE FIFTH

There were no bonfire night celebrations in Lewes or the Cliffe on 5 November. The Borough Bonfire Society made the first move towards cancellation on 24 October when it announced that it intended to postpone its programme to a future occasion 'on account of the illness in this town, and at the wish of numerous friends and subscribers, as well as the authorities of the borough'. It requested other societies to fall into line and this they did.

With the 'health of the town so improved' towards the end of November a suggested date for the celebrations was 2 December. However, the organisers were advised to wait a little longer as it was thought the excitement of the event might have a detrimental effect on partially recovered sufferers. The celebrations were eventually held on 30 December – on a clear, frosty night with a light covering of snow.

Cliffe becomes part of Lewes borough

1881

There was little enthusiasm in the Cliffe for the torchlight procession and fireworks with which Lewes celebrated the reading, on 22 June, of the charter of incorporation which Wynne Baxter, Lewes borough's last senior constable and first mayor, had collected from the Home Office.

Its inhabitants had petitioned the Privy Council against its proposed absorption into the new borough but the government commissioners appointed to consider its objections overruled them. The annual vestry of 25 March 1881 was the last occasion when Commissioners for Improving the Vill and Parish of the Cliffe were elected and in January 1882 the newly incorporated Lewes Borough Council formally accepted the transfer of property from them, including the Cliffe's fire engine, but 'without prejudging any questions with regard to its title and value'.

The following year some street names in the Cliffe were changed – North Street becoming Malling Street and East Street, Chapel Hill, to avoid confusion with similar directionally-named streets in Lewes. Some houses were re-numbered and others received numbers for the first time.

The rivalry between the two volunteer fire brigades became,

if anything, even more intense when they both came under the control of the new council. They seemed determined to continue as separate entities with their own fire stations, engines and equipment – and Cliffe insisted on retaining a residential qualification for membership. It was a situation which could not continue and in 1885 their captains were given two months to put forward the name of 'a gentleman willing to undertake the duties of Superintendent of the combined Borough Volunteer Fire Brigade'.

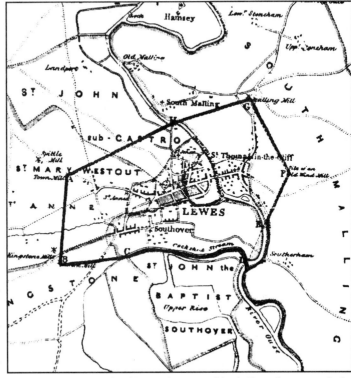

The redefined borough of Lewes, its extremities indicated, counterclockwise, by the letters A to H. A shaded line indicates the original borough boundary.

Parish room is extended

1884-1899

A 40ft by 22ft extension has been added to the parish room that was built fifty years ago to the north-west of St Thomas in the Cliffe.

The total cost of the new structure was £545 3s 10d and this amount has been raised by voluntary contributions. The extension will be used by the Sunday School and, if necessary,

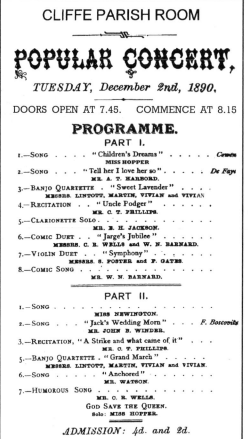

for a day school for the instruction of the children of poor parents. It also provides more much-needed space for meetings, lectures, concerts, and other activities on any day of the week except Sunday.

In the winter months popular concerts of songs, light music and recitations are held there. In April 1891, and again in January 1893 and February 1899 George Madgwick was granted a licence for one month by the council for the public performance of stage plays in the parish room. Perhaps some were by professional companies but surviving programmes of concerts show that the artists were local – and amateur – and seats were priced at fourpence and twopence.

The entertainment offered at South Malling schoolroom on 24 January 1888 was more up market. There were twenty-four items on the programme, including a reading by Mr Edmund Currey of Malling Deanery; songs from Mrs Cumberlege, Mrs Scamell, Miss Steggall and Miss L Smyth, who rendered, by request, a romantic ballad of the day, *The Bedouin Love Song*. Reserved seats were one shilling and the 'second seats' sixpence. Patrons were advised that 'carriages may be ordered at 9.45pm'.

FIRST FIRE AT BEAR YARD BEATS COMBINED BRIGADE

1886

The first major fire attended by the combined Cliffe/Lewes volunteer fire brigade under its new superintendent, James Pelling, started in a carpenter's shop in Bear Yard. It quickly spread from the ground to the first floor and to Strickland's corn store and stables, which were totally destroyed.

The brigade struggled for six hours to dowse the flames but the fire was not brought under control until the Brighton brigade, summoned by telegram, turned up with its steam-powered fire engine.

Golf takes over from cricket on Cliffe Hill

1896

The course today with a cluster of club buildings on the edge of Cliffe Hill.

Was it, perhaps, when they were playing or watching cricket on Cliffe Hill that some keen golfers noticed that the terrain formed a natural golf course? Notice it they did and sought permission from the tenant farmer, Thomas Wallis of Southerham, to play over it. Thomas Farncombe, whose family owned the *East Sussex News,* was one of these enterprising golfers and on 10 November 1896 that newspaper carried an advertisement announcing a meeting at the White Hart Hotel 'for the purpose of considering the formation of a golf club'.

Matters moved quickly. By the end of the month the newly-formed Lewes Golf Club had 103 members, each paying an entrance fee of a guinea and an annual subscription of the same amount; had leased the Cliffe Hill site for twenty-one years from the ground landlord, Lord Gage; and engaged a man to lay turf on the greens for 5½p an hour. He had been provided with an iron roller at a cost of £3 and two notice boards, acquired from Kemp Town Golf Club, had been put up warning about penalties for damaging the turf or club property.

Work of laying out a nine-hole course, designed by Thomas Gilroy, secretary of the Seaford Golf Club, started on 2 December and was completed by March 1897. The course was officially opened on 10 April, in splendid weather, with a match between the club's first professional, Harry Randall, and John Ross, professional of the Seaford Golf Club. Ross won.

Women were admitted to associate membership almost from the start, not for any reasons of equality but for the extra income. Golf was an expensive sport with its little white balls, so easily lost, each costing up to 2s 6d, and there was little prospect of any significant increase in membership without the ladies, God bless 'em. They could become associate members for 10s 6d a year and the subscription for 'Lady Visitors' was 2s 6d a week or a shilling a day.

Women were restricted to playing only on weekdays, and on the course they had to give way to the male members. They were not allowed to use the clubhouse which, as well as its 16ft by 14ft club room, had a dressing room, professional's workshop, steward's cupboard and, most importantly, a lavatory.

When the course was extended to eighteen holes in 1898 it was the end of cricket on Cliffe Hill. The pitch on which, since 1775, the summer game had been played, became the new second green of the golf course.

PUTTING THE CLOCK BACK

November 1889

The clock on St Thomas's church is now back in service after extensive repairs by Cliffe watchmaker William Tanner.

Cost of the work, said to be 'considerable', has been met by the parishoners.

Work starts on a memorial to the martyrs

11 October 1899

For the past ten years members of the committee formed to erect a memorial to the seventeen men and women of Sussex who were burnt for their faith outside the Star Inn, Lewes, in the sixteenth century have been trying to decide on a suitable site for it.

The ones suggested at the inaugural meeting in December 1889 were all as near as possible to the place of execution – either inside the entrance to the former Star Inn; at the top of School Hill; or in the form of a tablet and figures in bas relief over the entrance to the new town hall.

Today the foundation stone for the memorial was laid by Captain R Bingham RN on the western slope of Cliffe Hill – facing the site of the fire and visible from it. The land has been given by Lewes solicitor Isaac Vinall, son of the late Reverend John Vinall, minister of the Independent Calvinist Jireh Chapel which is at the foot of the hill. The secretary of the organising committee is Lewes postmaster Arthur Morris, another staunch and hard-working nonconformist.

Those attending the ceremony were invited to place money on the first of the 133 granite blocks that will form the 45ft 3ins high obelisk on which will be inscribed the names of the seventeen martyrs. In this way £49 was raised towards the £900 cost of the memorial, which took two years to build.

It had to be called Morris Road

20 March 1891

The layout of a new road of thirty houses – Nos 21-43 and 16-50 – behind the iron foundry that gave Foundry Lane its name, was today approved by Lewes council planners.

It is to be called, not surprisingly, Morris Road, after iron merchant Ebenezer Morris who lived for sixty-five years at 41 Cliffe High Street, which he rebuilt in 1828. It was there that he had his showroom; brought up thirteen children; and died in 1888, aged eighty-seven. Ebenezer Morris was chairman of the Board of Guardians of the Lewes Union for many years and at the time of his death was also chairman of the Lewes gas and water companies and a senior trustee of the Jireh Chapel.

5. THE UNEASY PEACE BETWEEN TWO WORLD WARS

1901-1950

The death of Victoria, Queen and Empress, on 22 January 1901 was a sombre start to the twentieth century. The day of her funeral, 2 February, was observed as a day of general mourning and all business was suspended. Memorial services were held in all the town's churches, the Free Churches holding a combined service in the Wesleyan Chapel and the Independent Calvinists marking the occasion with a service at the Jireh Chapel.

The inhabitants of the Cliffe and South Malling, still troubled by bad drains, recurring epidemics, a decline in waterborne trade and rising rate demands, found their new local authority intent on making life better for them, whether they liked it or not.

The mayor of Lewes, George Holman, set the tone for the future at a special council meeting held on 2 January. He said that he expected to see 'still greater improvements, more particularly in regard to sanitation and the laws of health and the physical and moral well-being of the people' than had already been achieved by the municipalities of the country. He was firmly of the opinion that 'dirt, disease and destitution would be driven out before the searchlight of sanitary science'. And indeed they were. Electric light was installed in Cliffe High Street and along Malling Street from Cliffe Corner to Thomas Street and the council borrowed £7,000 on the security of the General District Rates to provide a new sewerage system on the east side of the river, although a deputation of ratepayers claimed it was 'unnecessary and probably excessively expensive as well as being unsatisfactory in its working'.

The river in the 1920s. In the dinghies are, left, Lewes Rowing Club's steward, Edward Hylands and his son, Fred.

The area did not benefit from the rather more lively and less formal social life introduced by the accession of the card-playing, party-loving, horse-racing King Edward VII. It had no grand houses, only one racecourse, and no good shooting country in its immediate vicinity. At Malling Deanery Sir Frank Sanderson MP kept a low social profile and at Malling House the Bougheys enjoyed a quiet family life.

The First World War, which brought personal tragedies to many families, had little visible effect on the daily life of the community. The rector of St Thomas in the Cliffe, the Reverend Charles Snell, went off after Easter in 1917 to serve as an army chaplain, taking with him two presents from his parishioners – a portable altar and a 'lifesaving waistcoat'. The latter must have worked because he returned unharmed to the living a year later.

What did have a lasting effect, however, was

The Bear Hotel in its turn of the century heyday. Had the Automobile Association been in existence then – it was founded in 1905 but did not start rating accommodation until after the 1914-18 war – the Bear would probably have carried three stars.

the destruction of the Bear Hotel by fire in June 1918.

The 300-year-old hostelry was the Cliffe's principal meeting place. Generations of farmers had argued here over the price of wool; it had been the scene of balls to celebrate the famous victories; dinners to mark anniversaries, retirements, election successes; the inaugural and annual meetings of numerous recreational clubs and societies . . . The Court Leets of the Hundred of Ringmer had been held here, with all traditional formality; 'for two evenings only' in the eighteenth century. Mr Wildman had demonstrated his command of bees in its 'large commodious room' to a fascinated audience . . . It had stabling for forty horses and a number of carriages. There was a garage nearby for the sale, repair and maintenance of motor cars and boats could be hired for a leisurely row – on the flow up to Hamsey lock and back on the ebb. When it went there was nothing to take its place on this side of the river. Gentlemen and their ladies who wished to dine and dance had to cross the bridge, as did those with something to celebrate, meetings to conduct and improving talks to attend.

There were so many fires in the early 1900s that one wonders if there was a serial arsonist at work. Malling mill was reduced to ashes in 1908, three years later it was the turn of Thompsons the drapers in Cliffe High Street but that blaze was brought under control before too much damage was done. In September 1912 the Soap Factory Lane premises of corn and seed merchants Elphick and Son and contractor G B Kent were gutted.

There was little in the way of house building in the Cliffe and South Malling at this time. Lewes Portland Cement Company extended its operation from its works at South Heighton to the chalk pits in South Street and to Southerham but it was expanding to meet an increasing national rather than a local demand for building materials.

A new kind of shop appeared among the family-run butchers, bakers, chemists, newsagents, jewellers, clothing stores and fancy goods emporiums that lined each side of the High Street from Cliffe Corner to the bridge and spilled over into Malling Street and South Street. It was the multiple store – represented by provision merchants such as Lipton, the Maypole, the Home and Colonial, the International Stores, and, from 1929, by Woolworths with its wide variety of goods priced at either threepence or sixpence.

The traffic needing to cross the river, which had been a constant headache for the Cliffe for centuries, was still more four-legged than four-wheeled. Monday was market day and cows and sheep would make their way along Cliffe High Street to the sales ring opposite Lewes station. Shopkeepers would do their their best to protect their outdoor displays from the passing ruminants, and pedestrians would often help the drovers by forming a human barrier across the entrance to a side street or passageway to prevent a flock of sheep following their too-inquisitive leader down them.

Cattle had less curiousity, although on one hot summer's day a cow did walk through the open doorway of the World's Stores, pick her way delicately between the laden counters and, having inspected the goods on display, rejoined her sisters through the same open door, leaving only a trail of cow pats as evidence of her presence. A bullock being driven down Friars Walk to the abbattoir in North Court was less restrained. It charged at its own reflection in the window of Browne and Crosskey on the corner of School Hill, breaking the glass and ruining a display of the latest ladies' fashions

Change was, however, on the way. The engineering and technical skills learned in the 1914-18 war were put to good use in peacetime. Farmers began to drive tractors instead of teams of horses or oxen, the Austin Seven replaced the pony and trap, and the carriages of the rich were now chauffeur-driven Daimlers or Rolls Royces. Shops had vans as well as errand boys on bicycles for deliveries and heavy goods were carried round the country by lorries and freight trains rather than by ox cart, wagon or by barge.

The increase in mobility brought about by the internal combustion engine and a national railway system produced a new kind of traveller – the tourist and day tripper. The Cliffe and South Malling benefited little financially from these people. There were no longer show places like Baldy's Garden for them to visit. There were no beaches, no amusement arcades, no tea gardens – and the only hotel had burnt down. The cars and coaches carrying day trippers to the raffish delights of Brighton, and holidaymakers to the hotels of Eastbourne, rarely needed to use Cliffe bridge to cross the river. Neither did the day excursion coaches on their tours through the old world villages of downland and weald.

There was another technical step forward at the turn of the century that was of benefit to all but the career burglar – the installation of a mains supply of electricity, first to individual properties, and later on for street lighting. Another local authority initiative, completed by 1905, was the very necessary provision of main drainage in the Cliffe and South Malling.

The entrance to the Great Sewer, blocked by trees tidied up from the brewery and from the river frontage to Malling Brooks.
Photo: Bartlett Collection, Sussex Archaeological Society.

Cuilfail – the housing estate in a 'sheltered corner'

1901-10

The only private residential estate in the parish of St Thomas in the Cliffe is Cuilfail, on the south-facing slope of the hill above Malling Street. Plans for a coachhouse and stabling for the first house to be built there – it was on the north side of Chapel Hill and a little above Baldy's Garden – were approved in 1891.

The applicant and owner of the land was Lewes solicitor, Isaac Vinall. He continued his father's and grandfather's association with the Jireh Chapel by teaching in its Sunday school and for thirty years he was superintendent of the Lewes Ragged School.

Vinall became a member of the new council of the borough of Lewes in 1881 but two years later, when he was chairman of the finance and general purposes committee, he paid the statutory £15 fine and resigned his seat over a question that was then vexing the council. Should it, or should it not, buy the Corn Exchange and Star Hotel and convert the latter to a town hall?

The Finance Committee was in favour of going ahead with the purchase, but the council was split, and a poll of ratepayers showed a large majority against it.

In 1899 this property-developing solicitor gave a plot of land on his Cliffe hillside as a site for a memorial to the Protestant martyrs (see page 92). Invitations to the unveiling of the 210 ton obelisk on 11 October 1901 disclosed the name he had chosen for the estate. They granted guests: 'Admission to the Grounds of Cuilfail. . . ' He had named it *Cuilfail,* Gaelic for 'sheltered place', after the village of that name on the shores of Loch Melfort in Argyllshire where he and his family had spent several holidays.

After Isaac Vinall's death in 1907 at the age of sixty- four, the firm became Vinall and Sons, solicitors, of 220 High Street, Lewes and carried on the development of Cuilfail. Its first planning application was for a house for Lewis Vinall, Isaac's eldest son. It was to be called Melfort and its water supply would be from 'a private reservoir which has been tested and approved by the Medical Officer of Health'. By the end of the decade three more houses had been built and plans for a further four approved.

Although it rained all that afternoon 5,812 people climbed the hill to see the Countess of Portsmouth unveil the memorial.
Photo: Sussex Express.

Electric lighting up time

1901

Another utility serving the whole borough of Lewes has chosen to build its production plant in the Cliffe. In Bear Yard, only a few hundred yards by bird from the gas works at the bottom of Foundry Lane, is the new power house of the company that is to provide the private houses of the locality with electricity.

Building work in progress on the electricity company's power house in Bear Yard. Photo: Sussex Archaeological Society.

A 'model works arranged with mathematical correctness' has been set up by the Electrical Power Association Company on a one-acre site by the river. In the brick and iron premises, which were completed in May this year, are two large coal-fired steam engines coupled directly to dynamos which generate a low tension continuous current. The switchboard has gauges showing how much current is being used, on what lamps, and how much is in reserve.

The electricity produced goes to four distributing stations, three in Lewes and one in Malling Street, on the south side of the courtyard of the former White Swan coaching inn in Malling Street. From these a 220 volt supply is taken by underground cable to individual properties that are supplied with fuse boxes.

Electric street lighting came later. It had been called for by the inhabitants and talked about by the council since 1897 but it was not until the June 1900 that Lewes signed a contract with the Sussex Electric Power Distribution Company for it to be installed within two years in the main streets of the borough, including Cliffe High Street and along Malling Street to Thomas Street. By 1904 the work, costing £20,000, had been completed and the lamplighters who had walked around in all weathers with their long tapers to light the gas jets of the old street lights had lost their jobs.

POST OFFICE TRAGEDY
October 1900

Horace William Scrase, sub-postmaster at 14 Cliffe High Street since 1884, has died from a lethal dose of prussic acid.

Although no one was accused of any form of wrongdoing it is thought that the disappearance of a registered letter, said to contain £40 in gold coins, had been preying on his mind. The letter had been handed in on a January evening four years ago but was not in the registered postbag when it arrived the following morning at the sorting office.

Inhabitants blamed for drainage scheme delay

October 1905

In August 1901 the Local Government Board approved a loan of £6,290 16s 0d 'secured on the general rates' for the installation of mains drainage in the Cliffe and South Malling.

Work started in January 1903 and two years and ten months later it was completed 'at a total cost of £6,290 16s' proudly announced the chairman of the Cliffe Sewerage sub-committee, Cllr John Miles, to the council. He then suggested that the borough surveyor should be given £200 for his extra services as engineer for the scheme and for superintending the work.

This was not well received. Cllr Richard Hobden proposed the amount should be reduced to £100, arguing that the borough surveyor was hardly ever on site. 'The work would not have taken so long if it had been carried out by a competent man', he said and Cllr Arthur Green agreed:

'I live in the Cliffe and have had more opportunity than others to watch the works and for days the borough surveyor did not go near,' he said. 'Some of the drains were laid in trenches with water in them.' The sub-committee chairman put the blame for the delay on the people of the Cliffe rather than the borough surveyor.

'Unfortunately the council did not have the assistance from them it was entitled to,' he said. 'They put all sorts of obstacles in the way of the work that was being carried out.'

The amendment to halve the borough surveyor's bonus was lost by a large majority. That was not, however, the end of the affair. The council had to apply to the Local Government Board to borrow a further £300 to meet the cost of connecting all the houses serviced by the old culverts in the Cliffe to the new sewers.

A total of 306 connections have now been made, at a cost ranging from 6s 6d (32½p) to £40. The Board was told that there were a good many difficulties in the way of 'narrow streets, water-logged soil, etc – in fact,the Cliffe was a very difficult district altogether for the construction of sewerage works . . .'

UNION CONTINUES TO PAY OUTDOOR RELIEF

1903

A rate of 2d in the £ has, as usual, been levied by the council for the relief of the poor of the parish of St Thomas in the Cliffe. The old system of outdoor relief, which gave the needy a weekly allowance instead of putting them into the workhouse, has been continued by the Lewes Union. This year twenty-one people in the Cliffe were helped in this way. Thirteen of them were described as infirm, one asthmatic, one had imperfect sight, three were widowed, one a consumptive, one crippled and one had a broken thigh.

In the parish of South Malling there were eight in receipt of relief – one a widow with six children, four infirm, one paralysed, one blind, and one with heart disease.

Cement firm's wagon is a conversation stopper

c1905

This 6-ton monster – a Sentinel Standard undertype waggon built in 1907 – is a typical heavy goods vehicle of the period

The cement manufacturing company, started at South Heighton in 1884 by two Newhaven Harbour engineers has begun to work the Snowdrop chalk pit in South Street and the Southerham pit. Clay is brought up by river from the pits at Newhaven and mixed with chalk to get a Portland cement of a consistency to comply with the British Standard that was issued last year.

The arrival of the Lewes Portland Cement and Lime Company has proved to be a mixed blessing to the Cliffe. It has brought jobs to the area but it has also caused 'great inconvenience and nuisance' to the inhabitants with the heavy motor wagon it uses to take bags of cement to the railway station. The vehicle has also been involved in an accident with one of them. As it was coming out of the station yard it was in collision with a pony and trap driven by hairdresser and tobacconist James Bennett, who was on his way to his shop in Cliffe High Street. The shafts of the trap snapped and Bennett was thrown to the ground. He was bruised and shaken, but not seriously hurt.

Residents have complained to the council about the wagon. 'It is constructed of sheet iron which acts as a sounding board, and the vibration from it shakes down goods on display in shop windows,' they said. 'All conversation has to be suspended as it passes by.' When the complaint was passed on to the cement company it apologised profusely and offered to take any steps the council could suggest to stop the nuisance. 'The only remedy is for them to get another car, minus the objectionable features of the present one, and so live in goodwill with the inhabitants around them,' said Bridge Ward representative Cllr Gerard Lloyd.

Presumably this is what the company did for there were no more complaints.

LAMP CAUSES DAIRY FIRE
1 September 1905

A passerby noticed smoke coming from premises of the Danish Dairy Company on Thursday evening. He broke in through the half glass door and found a bicycle with its front oil lamp still alight and its front tyre burning.

TOP MARKS
9 March 1905

A school inspector's report was received at Malling Parochial School today with 'much cheering' for it stated: 'It would be difficult to praise too highly the tone and character of the training given in this painfully overcrowded school.'

There is a cluster of pubs in Cliffe High Street – the Bear Hotel, the Cliffe Tavern, the Castle and beyond it, without a sign, the Gardeners Arms, opposite which is the Beehive beerhouse.

Six beerhouses are closed down

1907

Cliffe has lost six of its nine beerhouses and for a few weeks, between the Brewster Sessions and Quarter Sessions, the future of a seventh, the Gardeners Arms, was in doubt. The police opposed the renewal of the licences, not because any of the houses were badly run but because they were in clusters.

The only one of its nine fully-licensed houses to go was the Old Ship, 55 yards away from the Thatched House in South Street, which also lost its Anchor beer-house.

Malling Street lost the Tanners Arms, which had average sales of 112 barrels a year and was 37 yards away from the fully-licensed Wheatsheaf; and the Hare and Hounds and the Foresters Arms – both close to each other and to the Dorset Arms and the Swan.

Cliffe Tavern in Cliffe High Street, which sold an average of seventy-seven barrels of beer a year and was within 20 yards of the Bear Hotel and 43 yards from the Castle, had its renewal application refused but that of its near neighbour, the Gardeners Arms, was granted. At Quarter Sessions, where the final decisions to renew or refuse were made and compensation agreed, it was described as 'a well-conducted house aver-aging sales of 184 barrels and a 100 dozen bottled beers.'

Court agrees: 'Betting on horses is not gaming'

1908

The Swan Inn in Malling Street, owned by Beard's brewery, came close to losing its licence at the March Brewster Sessions because the licensee, Mrs Mary Keep had, on 21 January the previous year, been fined £5 with £1 8s costs for permitting gambling on the premises.

The 'gamblers' were two Brighton police officers who had visited the Swan, a house which did a big trade particularly with carriers of goods to nearby towns and villages. When the officers had made bets on some horses, Mrs Keep, who was a widow, was charged with allowing them to do so and was waiting for her appeal against her conviction to be heard. 'There is the question of entrapment to be investigated and it has always been recognised that a licensee had to have three convictions before renewal was refused,' it was said by the brewery's solicitor on her behalf.

The licensing justices accepted Mrs Keep's undertaking that she would leave the Swan if her appeal was refused and they renewed the licence.

At Quarter Sessions a month later the brewey was represented by leading advocate, Sir Edward Marshall Hall. He successfully argued that betting on horses was not gaming and the appeal was allowed, but with no order as to costs.

Prompt action by neighbours saves the Jireh Chapel

15 March 1907

Prompt action by neighbours with buckets of water and two firemen with a hose cart put out a fire that could, had it not been checked, have spread quickly through the all-wood interior of the Jireh Chapel on Wednesday morning.

The outbreak was confined to an area by the staircase leading to the gallery where there had been an escape of gas from a pipe near the meter for several days. The gas had mysteriously caught light and it had produced a jet of flame so fierce that it melted the surrounding copper pipes and caused an estimated £60 to £70 worth of damage. The gas supply has now been cut off by plugging the main outside and it has been decided to hold Sunday's services in the Sunday School.

SACKED DUSTMAN'S SUICIDE

17 February 1905

Losing his job on the council dust carts caused Alfred Towner, aged sixty-five, to take his own life. He was found with his throat cut in a shed at the back of his house in Thomas Street last week. His wife, Harriett, told the coroner that her husband, who had lost an eye two years ago while emptying a dust hole for the council, had taken to lying in bed until lunch time in the five weeks since he had been laid off work. He had gone out into the yard at 5.30am complaining of pains in his head. She found him in the shed and called the doctor but he died an hour later. The verdict of the inquest held at the Dorset Arms was 'suicide during temporary insanity'.

TIDY – BUT DO NOT TOUCH

22 March 1907

Cliffe churchwardens were authorised by the vestry to keep the two disused parish burial grounds in Malling Street in order. They must not, however, touch the gravestones as these are private property.

HORSES GIVE WAY TO STEAM
1906

Harvey's Brewery is replacing its horse-drawn delivery drays with steam wagons. First to go into service was a Foden with wooden wheels, solid rubber tyres and a legal top speed of 8mph.

If more load space was needed one of the old drays – without the horses – would be attached to a towing hitch at the rear.

❖ ❖ ❖

PUPILS HAVE NO SHOES
31 January 1908

Poor parents are keeping their children away from Malling primary school because they cannot afford to buy them shoes to wear.

The headmistress, Miss Kate Fowler-Tutt, is appealing for discarded footwear of any size that she can distribute to her poorest pupils. 'Parcels will be collected if the donors send me a postcard,' she says in a letter to the *East Sussex News*.

❖ ❖ ❖

NEW VICAR
1908

The new vicar of St Michael's, Malling, is the Reverend Robert Marriott who has recently returned from service as a missionary in Bengal.

❖ ❖ ❖

Malling windmill is burned down

8 September 1908

A windmill that caused the death of a woman with its sweeps; fractured the skull of a grinder hoisting sacks by dropping tackle on him; and drew his brother into its machinery and broke his arm, has burned down. Only in one accident did the mill come off worst. A sweep broke off when it hit, but did not hurt, a grazing cow.

A Corporation carter saw a column of black smoke coming from the mill at 11.30am and rode on his horse to the fire station to alert the brigade. When the firemen arrived with the steamer and manual engines the mill was blazing from top to bottom and flames were rising to a height of 100ft. The only water available was from two small reservoirs and by the time 1,000 gallons had been poured onto the fire without any effect it was decided to let the old post mill burn itself out.

There has been a mill on Malling Hill certainly since 1625 and deeds in the possession of the Sussex Archaeological Society show it was worked in that year by John Bayley and John Kenner.

Cliffe baker, Frank Stone, was the last to use it for grinding corn and it was he who installed a gas engine in the roundhouse for chaff cutting in 1900.

The mill, which was insured, is now owned by Mr Castle Leaver of Brighton, the proprietor of the nearby Lewes Sanitary Steam Laundry which had its painted weatherboarding blistered by the heat from the blazing windmill.

The roundhouse of Malling's post mill survived the fire and was converted to a private house.

Competitors prepare to be towed in their flat- bottomed craft from the Bear Hotel's landing stage to the start at Glynde Reach.
Photo: Bartlett Collection.

A boat race between bridges . . .

April 1908

On Good Friday there was a flat-bottomed boat race on the Ouse from Sound Bridge, where the Glynde Reach leaves the main river, to Cliffe Bridge, a distance of two-and-a-half miles. Henry Baker, who had a ten minute start for reasons not disclosed by the *East Sussex News* in its report of the event, carried the Cambridge colours to victory in a time of thirty-seven minutes. He was nearly beaten in the last half mile by Tom Thorpe who finished half a minute behind him. In the afternoon there was a greasy pole climbing contest and the winner was William Costick. Organiser of the water sports was Harry Nash, manager of the butcher's shop at 9 Cliffe High Street. The prizes were distributed at a smoking concert at the Bear Shades on Monday evening.

. . . and a barrow race round the town

There are several versions of the wheelbarrow race that started from outside the Thatched House in South Street on a May evening in 1910. One is that two of the pub's regulars pushed miniature wheelbarrows to the top of Cliffe Hill and back for a barrel of beer and the loser suffered a minor heart attack.

Another version is that James Bowles met a stranger at the Thatched House who wagered a gallon of beer that he could beat him in a wheelbarrow race round the town. Bowles was expecting a full-sized barrow but the stranger produced two toy ones. Both contestants were exhausted after trundling them up School Hill to St Michael's church in the High Street and back. The unnamed winner collapsed and could not celebrate his victory so his friends drank the beer.

A third version is that Jimmy Bowles, aged fifty, won the race but his opponent was broke so could not produce the £5 he had wagered on the result.

Early risers to the rescue

23 February 1911

Surprisingly a number of people were walking along Cliffe High Street in the early hours and noticed that Thompsons drapers' shop was on fire. A police officer on patrol called the fire brigade at 3.30am, and fireman Fuller, who was passing the shop window at about the same time, dashed round to the Cliffe fire station – a few yards away on the east side of St Thomas's church. He grabbed a hose reel and had water playing on the blaze on the ground floor for a full minute before the brigade arrived at 3.36am. Others who were on hand to help to safety the twelve people who had been asleep in their beds in rooms above the shop, were two other police officers and lamplighter, Edwin Fuller. They had heard the sound of breaking glass and hastened to the scene. The fire was put out before it could do serious harm to the building or spread to neighbouring properties.

Steamer's crew has to wait for the horses

9 September 1912

The horses that pulled the brigade's engines were on other council work when a fire that did an estimated £1,700 worth of damage broke out at the Soap Factory Lane premises of Elphick and Son and contractor G B Kent in at 2pm today. The steamer's crew had to wait for twenty minutes for the animals to be unhitched from a rubbish cart on the outskirts of the

town before the appliance could drive to the fire. Although water was pumped from the river as well as from a hydrant in the lane the fire had too firm a hold for the buildings to be saved. The flames had been fuelled by the contents of kegs of molasses that had dripped on to the bales of hay stored beneath them.

Barges are still delivering the goods

1920s

A loaded barge with sail set makes its slow way upstream from Newhaven.

In spite of increasing competition from the railway there was plenty of water-borne trade on the Ouse in the first two decades of the new century. An occasional sea-going vessel would require the bridge at Southerham to be opened but barges were the principal carriers of cargo. Clay was brought upstream almost daily to the Lewes Portland Cement Company's dock on the east bank at Southerham and to its wharf in South Street which could take craft of up to 9ft draught.

Corn and seed merchants Elphick and Son had their own fleet of four barges – *Samuel, Charlotte, Rebecca and Bessie,* all named after members of the family – operating from their wharf on the Great Sewer at the end of Soap Factory Lane.

Berry and Bussey of South Malling had, every year since 1828, brought some 6,500 tons of coal from Newhaven to the gas works in Foundry Lane. Sometimes, on neap tides, the two-man crews poling the coal barges upstream with 12ft long quants had to unload some of their cargo into the river to save their craft grounding below the bridge at Southerham. Whenever this happened the local lads would collect as much of the discarded coal as they could from the mud at low water to augment their families' supply of winter fuel. It was not until 1927, when the gas company went over to a new system of production, that it had its coal supplies delivered by rail.

TOP DOG
1913

Harry Nash, manager of W and R Fletcher, butchers, of 9 Cliffe High Street, is also a successful dog breeder. His spaniel, Cliff Banker by Flash Fashion out of Cliff Figet has, at his first three shows gained five firsts, two specials, three seconds and one third and reserve championship. He was also best-in-show dog at the Shrewsbury Royal Championship show.

A BONFIRE SOCIETY FOR THE CHILDREN
1913

The bonfire societies in Lewes were for adults only until Tom Wheeler thought that it would be a good idea if children were allowed to take part. Not only would they enjoy it, they would also learn about the traditions of bonfire and how to make torches, build tableaux and deal with fireworks. So, with the help of some like-minded friends, Tom formed the South Street Juvenile Bonfire Society and this year, for the first time, torches were carried in procession by adults and children in fancy dress to a bonfire behind the Thatched House.

The First World War

1914-1918

On Tuesday 4 August at 11pm Britain and Germany were at war. The catalyst to the conflict was the assassination of Austrian Archduke Francis Ferdinand by a Serbian student at Sarajevo on 28 June.

The causes went back further and were more complex. Scientific advances and the development of new machinery had made mass production possible and created great wealth for European industrialists. To safeguard their new-found prosperity they imposed tariff barriers to limit foreign competition and their workers, eager for better wages and working conditions, supported them. This led to a fierce nationalism and

The Maypole Dairy in wartime with BUSINESS AS USUAL signs on either side of a shield showing the flags of the Allies.
Photo: Bartlett Collection, Sussex Archaeological Society.

the formation of power blocs, both economic and military, with the Balkans as the powder keg.

After Sarajevo there were frenzied diplomatic moves to keep the peace but when Russia and Austro-Hungary mobilised their forces against Serbia, and Germany sent troops into the Grand Duchy of Luxembourg whose neutrality it had guaranteed, war was inevitable.

There was little thought of war in the Cliffe and South Malling over the Bank Holiday weekend. Members of the Lewes Rowing Club were busy in the boatyard in South Street preparing their craft for the Venetian fete to be held at the Pells and Saturday shoppers found that another multiple store, the Maypole Dairy Company, had opened a branch in Cliffe High Street next to the sub-post office and stationers run by Mrs Scrase. And they would hardly have missed noticing the big new display window in Frederick Tickner's china and glass shop, next to the outfitters run by his brother, Sidney.

There had been a change of management at the Bear Hotel, Mr and Mrs Thomas Dulake taking over from Mrs Edith Bagshaw. However, Mrs Edith Baker was still pulling pints at the Gardeners Arms and Henry Newnham doing the same across the road at the Beehive. Many of the young men drinking their beer that weekend would soon be on their way to the killing fields of France and Flanders, or to serve on the high seas with the British

Fleet. They would not be conscripts, there was no conscription until 1916. They would volunteer to go – and few would come home.

The fact that Britain was on the brink of war was not mentioned in pre-Bank Holiday editions of the *Sussex Express.* However, on Friday 6 August it told its readers about the war. Not on the front page, that was for advertisements; or page two, that had the score cards of cricket matches played over the holiday; or page three, the Home Page with drawings of the latest in ladies' corsetry. On page four, headlined: GREAT SCENE AT LEWES, was a photograph of soldiers about to board a train. It was, said the paper: 'Town's farewell to Territorials as they depart on Wednesday afternoon.' Not until readers reached page seven did they learn why the Territorials were departing. Beneath the four-decker headline:

ENGLAND AT WAR
Germany's Isolated Defiance
REAL PATRIOTISM AT HOME
An appeal to the men and women of Sussex

were all four verses and chorus of what was described as '*A Marching Song* by A Ward Higgs'. It is sung today, but rarely in its entirety, at civic and festive occasions throughout the county as *Sussex by the Sea.*

There was little hard news in the rest of the two columns occupied by the war story. Readers were informed that a small crowd had gathered outside Lewes Post Office on Tuesday night waiting to learn by telegram

of Germany's answer to Britain's ultimatum regarding the neutrality of Belgium. The railway was being guarded by the military and 'men with fixed bayonets do duty night and day at bridges and tunnels around the district'.

Within a matter of days, however, everyone in the area was made only too well aware of the war by the physical presence of some 10,000 men on their way to France to become part of the 150,000-strong British Expeditionary Force under the command of Sir John French. They were encamped on downland and billeted in church halls and houses. Then, as suddenly as they had come they were gone, sailing from Newhaven to face a 500-gun bombardment from the Germans at Mons on 24 August.

There were no dramatic interruptions to daily life in the Cliffe and South Malling in the next four years with the exception of an unprecendented action by the British Army. It closed a pub. The White Swan in Malling Street, which started its licensed life as the King and Queen in the seventeenth century, was a favourite haunt of the Canadians billeted in the neighbourhood. One night some British Tommies made a takeover bid for the premises. Tempers flared, fists flew and at the end of the affray a Canadian soldier was found dead from stab wounds on the doorstep. There were mutterings among the Canadians about revenge and to prevent further trouble the licensee, Samuel Moon, was ordered to close for the duration. The White Swan never opened as an inn again.

Elizabeth Bennett was two months away from her seventh birthday when the war started and was living with her parents in Morris Road. In 1997 she published *My Memories of Lewes Over Many Years* and says of those wartime days: 'Many men were called for service and women took their places in shops places in shops and offices and factories doing their best to carry on and keep smiling. Supplies in the shops were low and were used sparingly . . .'

Ladies of the parish collecting outside St Thomas's church on St George's Day for comforts for the troops.
Photo: Richard Philcox.

A *Memorandum as to Air Raids* was issued by the Chief Constable, Major Hugh Lang, in 1915. It advised people not to go into the streets during a raid as they might be struck by falling missiles; to keep buckets of water and sand on upper floors so any small fires could be easily dealt with; and to keep all lower-floor

Volunteer nurse Jessie Page in her uniform.
Photo: Richard Philcox.

windows and doors closed to prevent the admission of noxious gases.

'An indication that poison gas is being used will be that a peculiar and irritating smell may be noticed following the dropping of a bomb,' states the memorandum, and sug-

gests that 'the nose and mouth should be covered with a pad of cotton waste soaked in a solution of washing soda should a gas attack occur'.

In the Cliffe and South Malling no bombs were dropped, no poison gas was released. The inhabitants were spared the physical horrors of a war that claimed the lives of more than ten million of its combatants. But they were not spared the deep agony of loss . . .

THE PARISH REMEMBERS THEM

The names of forty seven men of the parish of St Thomas in the Cliffe who made the supreme sacrifice are inscribed in six columns on a memorial tablet of Sussex marble. It is on the altar in the south aisle of the church and was erected in 1920 and paid for by the parishioners.

TO THE GLORY OF GOD IN MEMORY OF THE MEN OF THIS PARISH WHO GAVE THEIR LIVES IN THE GREAT WAR 1914-1918

D J CARPENTER	H S BOLLING	P CHAMPION	A ELDRIDGE	C R COOMBES	E RICHARDSON
W G COOMBES	R COWLES	S CRICK	W H HARRIS	W RUSSELL	F H TRIGWELL
F TRIGWELL	W P CRIPS	C DEACON	L J HAYLER	E LARKIN	C STREETER
H M BRIDGER	C C WELLER	T E JENNER	A J RAWARD	A MITCHELL	H BATCHELOR
J WOOD	A J JONES	D C WALKER	C MILHAM	A GASTON	P E BRIDGER
F J HOLMAN	F W BRIDGER	W STEDMAN	J THORPE	C F FROST	W RUSSELL
I SKINNER	G W HUTSON	P A RUSSELL	E IZZARD	H V MANN	H N AUSTIN
N WELCH	W T PAGE	J SHORT	R HARVEY	W HOAD	

The £25,000 Bear Hotel blaze

15 July 1918

The scene of devastation on the morning after the fire.

The 300-year-old Bear Hotel and two corn stores were destroyed by a fire that broke out in the early hours of Tuesday morning. The proprietor's wife, Mrs Tom Dulake, was awakened by the smell of smoke and her husband ran into their son's room at the back of the house and found its window frame on fire. He roused the nine hotel guests and five members of staff and everyone left hurriedly in their night clothes, leaving behind all their personal possessions.

When the fire brigade arrived the garage in Bear Yard was burning fiercely and flames had spread to the hotel on one side and to Strickland's granary on the other side. Because of the neap tide the river was at an unusually low level and the only source of water was from a hydrant 200 yards away in Foundry Lane. The fire continued to spread, first to Rice Brothers cycle shop and other premises behind the hotel. As soon as one of these outbreaks was put out another started and the situation became even more serious when Stevenson's warehouse on the opposite side of the river caught alight.

Luckily, at about this time the Brighton brigade arrived with its motor fire engine, connected up to a hydrant on School Hill and was able to concentrate its jets on the burning buildings on the town side. There was help, too, for the Lewes brigade from the Brighton Railway fire brigade, which came with its engine on the 6.20am train. Newhaven Railway brigade's tug *Hauler* went aground at Sound Bridge on its way up river and grounded again opposite the gas works from where hoses were run out over four barges to direct water onto the blazing buildings on the Cliffe side. The combined efforts of the brigades had the fire under control by 8.30am but it was not extinguished until midday.

Damage to the hotel and to the surrounding buildings has been estimated at £25,000. The personal belongings of the hotel's guests and staff were completely destroyed, as were the two cars and a motorcycle in the garage and the corn, hay and straw in the warehouses. The footbridge linking them collapsed from the Cliffe side and the heat in Stevenson's warehouse was so intense that the iron columns supporting its four storeys melted, sending hundreds of mice scuttling out into the road. Helpers at the scene led horses from the livery stables to safety, and rescued a sitting hen and some rabbits that were kept in a hutch on the hotel balcony.

Harvey's Brewery was one of a number of business premises in Cliffe High Street damaged by floodwater which, after days of heavy rain in January 1925, drained from the Downs and caused the Ouse to burst its banks.
Photo: Bartlett Collection, Sussex Archaeological Society.

Traders want an opening bridge – not a bypass

5 December 1924

Cliffe residents and traders have been asking for some time for a new bridge across the Ouse. They want one that can be opened to allow vessels to pass through and provide a flatter profile for road users. East Sussex County Council, which since its formation in 1888 has been responsible for the bridge, has suggested building a bypass instead, to take traffic away from the High Street. This is a revival of a scheme put forward by Lewes borough a century ago, and one that caused the Cliffe, then a separate township, to obtain an Act of Parliament in 1837 and widen its own main street by nine feet.

'It has infuriated every shopkeeper and trader in Cliffe High Street and Malling Street', said Colonel C Cheeswright, vice president of the Cliffe Social Club. 'They are, without exception, most emphatic that such a bypass road would ruin their trade.'

A year later the county suggested removing the present bridge and replacing it with a flatter non-opening one but the town was against this scheme because it would restrict the size of craft using the river, and cause great inconvenience to one of its major industries – Cllr John Every's Phoenix Iron Works. Instead it wanted improvements made to the present bridge and promised to consider 'any reasonable suggestion for a contribution towards the cost'.

Five years later the town got its way and in July 1931 work on improving the existing bridge began. However the council went back on its promise to consider contributing towards the cost on the grounds that the Ministry of Transport's grant towards the work would be proportionately reduced and borough ratepayers would be contributing to the scheme in common with other ratepayers in the county.

The new gas holder at the southern end of Morris Road.

Engineers from Norway visit reconstructed gas works

September 1928

Two deputations, one from Stavanger, the other from Bergen, have visited the reconstructed gas works in Foundry Lane to see for themselves the revolutionary vertical retort system of gas production that has been installed there.

The retorts can use unscreened Durham coal, which is cheap and easily obtainable. 'Hitherto the use of this coal in vertical retorts was not considered practical by engineers,' says the gas company in its half-yearly report.

The installation, which includes a new gas holder, is working satisfactorily and is providing the town with more gas from less coal, and at a more satisfactory pressure.

The success of the new system accounts for the interest of the engineers from Scandinavia where there are abundant supplies of unscreened coal.

'NO PAY' RATES PROTEST

20 April 1928

As a protest about the state of the road leading from the Steam Laundry to his house in Malling Field a member of the Lewes Board of Guardians has refused to pay his rates.

Thomas Emerson, who owes a total of £10 12s 2d – £5 15s.0d poor rate and £4 17s 2d general district rate – told the court that he had never before refused to pay his rates but he wanted to draw attention to the dilapidated state of the road.

The magistrates' clerk, E Lawson Lewis, pointed out that if the authorities were not discharging their liabilities in respect of the road he may possibly have a case against them.

'Representations have been made to them but they try to get out of it by the back door, saying the road does not belong to them,' replied Mr Emerson.

He said that he was prepared to pay what he owed 'now I have made my protest'.

GUIDEBOOK'S ADVICE IS: 'NEGLECT THE CLIFFE'

1928

Novelist and playwright F Frankfort Moore of Castlebank House, Lewes has some unkind things to say about the Cliffe in his recently-published guide, *A Few Hours in Lewes*. He describes it as 'a low-lying, narrow thoroughfare mostly of small shops' with the church as 'the only building of interest to the casual visitor'.

'To reach it one must descend a steep hill, weighted down with the reflection that it must be surmounted later on,' he writes. 'I think that the Cliffe and Malling Street should be carefully neglected.'

The width of Cliffe bridge is being doubled by the addition of a second span of the same size and shape as that of the old bridge.

Ancient ford found beneath the river bed

July 1931

Workmen excavating foundations for the widening of Cliffe bridge have come across the remains of what may have been the ford across which Henry III's defeated troops fled after the Battle of Lewes in 1264. On each bank, 10ft below the surface and about a foot below the present river bed, a 12in-thick road made of small flints and what looks like ashes, has been uncovered. Also found there was an ornamental knife, a medieval horseshoe, a pewter plate and several cast iron cannon balls. Mr J C H Martin, who has garage premises on the former Bear Hotel site as well as on the Lewes side of the river, is having two of the cannon balls mounted in frames made of old timbers and intends to present them to the Sussex Archaeological Society's museum.

The 130ft-long bridge is being doubled to a width of 39ft to provide a 25ft carriageway edged on each side with 7ft-wide pavements, and the sum of £5,000 has been allocated for the work. A new arch of exactly the same size, height and shape is being added to the seaward side. It will have a concrete rim and lining and be faced with the original red bricks and be bordered by the stone curb and vertical iron railings from the old bridge. A length of the town wharf on the west bank has had to go to make room for the new span and its landing stage and steps are being built further to the south.

The work was completed by October 1932 but not to the total satisfaction of the town council. It complained about the 'unsatisfactory and dangerous state' of the new paving, for which the county blamed the weather. 'Pedestrians could not be turned off the narrow pavements and they stood on the slabs when the foundations were wet,' it said.

Church celebrates its tercentenary

St Michael the Archangel, South Malling commemorated its re-building in 1628 and re-consecration on 24 May 1632 by inviting subscriptions to a number of funds for the future.

Contributions were sought for:

a) immediate repairs to the church fabric

b) to form a small capital fund for future repairs, and

c) to provide a peal of tubular bells.

Throughout its history the little church that replaced the edifice in which the secular canons of the Collegiate Church of St Michael the Archanagel worshipped, has maintained its evangelical character. The first incumbent was the Puritan Esdras Coxall and the living is now in the gift of the low church Martyrs Memorial and Church of England Trust. Until 1926 the advowson was in private hands – and these were, with a few exceptions, the owners of Malling Deanery.

Sir Frank Sanderson, who not did take on the advowson when he bought the Deanery in 1924, has transferred a piece of its garden to the vicarage – formerly Deanery Garden Cottage. In return the Ecclesiastical Commissioners have given £100 as capital to the benefice. By 1929 enough money had been raised to replace the church's single bell by a carillon of eight tubular bells. These have to be played from a keyboard and for the next fifty-three years they were, every Sunday before morning and evening services, by Arthur Constable who lived over the river in Toronto Terrace and worked for Beard's Brewery.

COUNTY BUYS CORNER SHOPS

26 February 1932

Three shops on Cliffe Corner – a butchers' and Shaw's grocers at 2 and 4, Malling Street – have been bought for £2,200 by East Sussex County Council. They are to be pulled down as part of a scheme to widen 'this narrow and dangerous thoroughfare'.

NEW RECTORY

1930

Cliffe rectors, who have shared the 1 Albion Street, Lewes rectory of All Saints parish since 1799, when their parsonage in North Street was demolished, now have one of their own again. An 'exchange of rectories' has taken place at a cost of £2,687 19s 1d, and 21 Malling Street, opposite the Dorset Arms, has been bought by the diocese.

SERGEANT'S STOP AND SEARCH CATCHES A THIEF IN POSSESSION

19 August 1932

On his way from Lewes to investigate a report he had 'received by telephone' from the licensee, Percival Burr, of a break-in and theft of cigarettes from the Fox Inn at Southerham a police officer chanced to meet, and arrest, one of the thieves.

Police Sergeant Childey was cycling down South Street when he saw a youth walking towards him. He decided to stop and search the young man and found all ten packets of the missing cigarettes in his pockets, together with a nail which had been used to force open a cupboard in the bar. The nineteen-year-old was from London and had come down for the weekend with a friend.

Gala opening of a super cinema

The Art Deco arch on the arcade entrance to the new super cinema, designed by Andrew Mather.
Photo: Sussex Express

2 June 1934

Two years ago 34 Cliffe High Street, a Georgian house with columns to its shop front, pictured below, was demolished. It has now been replaced by a 986-seater Odeon cinema providing 'perfect sound, a brilliant picture' and a free car park in South Street.

There was a full house for the gala opening by Viscount Gage but the 'noted film stars who have promised to attend' did not do so.

However, the chairman, Oscar Deutsch, after whom the cinema chain – '**O**scar **D**eutsch **E**ntertains **O**ur **N**ation – is named, was there, together with his fellow directors. The 486 seats in the circle were occupied by leading residents of the town, who were guests of the management. The feature film was *Aunt Sally* starring Cicely Courtneidge, together with a Silly Symphony and the popular comic duo, Laurel and Hardy, in *Me and My Pal*. Patrons were entertained in the interval; by Leslie Haskell and his Band. The Odeon is open on weekdays from 2.15pm. Seats are priced at 7d, 1s, 1s 6d and 2s.

ARCHBISHOP'S NAME WAS NOT THOMAS À BECKET

19 February 1933

All too often the martyred Archbishop of Canterbury, to whom Cliffe church is dedicated, is wrongly named. It is as much a national as a local error as Mr C J Cox of Birmingham points out in expressing his surprise, in a letter to today's *Observer*. 'Why does this popular error die so hard?' he asks. 'The archbishop was the son of Gilbert Becket and was called by his contemporaries Thomas of London and when archbishop, so referred to himself'.

In Strype's *Cranmer* the point is made with even more vigour:'This is a small error but being so often repeated deserveth to be observed and corrected. The Name of that Archbishop was Thomas Becket nor can it otherwise be found to have been written in any Authentick History, Record, Kalendar or other Book. If the Vulgar did formerly, as it doth now, call him Thomas a Becket their Mistake is not to be followed by Learned Men.'

The Shamrock jammed by the bows beneath Cliffe bridge.

An end to water-borne trade

16 March 1937

The Ouse has ceased to be a commercial waterway of any great consequence. Clay from Piddinghoe is now delivered by road to Eastwoods, which took over the Lewes Portland Cement Company in 1929. The Cliffe Great Sewer has started to silt up and the south east spur is being filled in.

One of the last sea-going sailing barges to use the river was the *Shamrock*. She was a regular visitor to Every's wharf and on 5 March she berthed there with a cargo of steel from Belgium. Ten days later she was being poled downstream stern first, with her mast and rigging lowered to deck level, and had almost cleared Cliffe bridge when a large pulley in her bows jammed against the northern arch. The 87ft by 21ft by 7ft barge stuck fast and the incoming tide lifted her up against the bridge. To relieve this pressure Lewes Fire Brigade pumped 10,000 gallons of water into her empty holds and pumped it out again when the tide ebbed. *Shamrock* was finally freed in the late afternoon and the following day she was towed to Newhaven by Ted Gillam in his 20ft fishing boat *Our Johnnie,* which was powered by a 12hp diesel engine. From the harbour mouth at Newhaven to Lewes is an eight-and-a- quarter-mile trip. An upstream tow on the flood, downstream on the ebb, cost 25s and took between one-and a-half to two hours.

The *Shamrock*, built at Sittingbourne in 1899, ended her days as a ballast barge at Barnstable. In the 1950s she was hulked.

A RARE ACCESSORY TO WORSHIP
1936

The entry for: LEWES, ST THOMAS CANTUAR in a survey of 'Ancient Church Accessories to Divine Worship . . . in the Diocese of Chichester' published this year under the title: *The Treasures of Sussex Churches* includes its four-teenth century double squint. It was cut through what was then an outer wall of the Norman chapel of ease so that lep- ers could take part in the Mass and see the elevation of the Host without coming into contact with members of the congregation. It now provides a view of the chancel from the north-west wall of the south aisle.

There is a similar double squint at Rodmell, referred to in the *Victoria County History, vol 2* as 'another of these peculiar squints, divided in two by a mid-wall shaft of plain character'.

The cameraman of the Cliffe

Henry John Bartlett 1865–1947

Photography was the hobby of Henry John Bartlett and from the quality of his work, of which these pictures of new shops in Cliffe High Street is an example, it could have well been his profession. He was initially employed by the Lewes Gas, Light and Coke Company to empty its customers' meters and bring the coins in a square metal case to its offices in Foundry Lane. He later joined the staff of Hillman and Sons, solicitors, of 221 High Street and in the 1920s his name appears regularly in newspaper reports of the gas company's half-yearly meetings as proposer or seconder of various motions.

Staff of food shops in the Cliffe pose outside their premises for Harry Bartlett's camera. The International Stores opened for business at 3 Cliffe High Street in and below, Eastmans 1922 Christmas display.

Harry Bartlett lived at 14 Morris Road, one of a group of new houses built by Edward Milham in the early 1900s. It was called Primrose after the Primrose League – formed in 1883 for the dissemination of Conservative principles – of which his wife, Beatrice, was a member.

When not at work he was out and about with his camera. The results of these forays are the 200 or so photographs of new public utililty buildings, shop fronts, street scenes and civic occasions that form the Sussex Archaeological Society's Bartlett Collection.

A further 700 glass plates have recently been given to East Sussex Record Office and they show more of the commercial side of Bartlett's work. There are studio-style photographs of children with teddy bears and toys, families in their Sunday best, happy couples in their wedding finery and one of a splendid granny in black bombazine,

lips drawn in upon toothless gums. There are fashion photographs of severe looking women modelling tea gowns and men posing self-consciously in suits.

In contrast are the First World War pictures of soldiers in camp, on manoeuvres, and a contingent crossing Cliffe bridge with light machine guns strapped to their bicycles.

The tall, well dressed solicitor's clerk was also a keen cyclist and grower of vegetables. His Morris Road neighbour, Miss Elizabeth Bennett,

From the turn of the century Lipton was the name on the fascia of 41 Cliffe High Street, formerly showrooms of ironfounder Ebenezer Morris.

remembered well the ritual performed by the Bartletts every time they mounted their tandem and set off for their allotment which was 'off the Offham Road'. She describes it in her book, *My Memories of Lewes Over Many Years*:

> Mrs Bartlett always dressed in a red suit trimmed with black braid and pillbox hat to match. Mr Bartlett would place the tandem by the kerb and get on the back seat and his wife in front and would say '1-2-3 go' and off they went . . .

Harry Bartlett retired in 1939. 'When his wife died he missed her very much but carried on in the same way and still grew vegetables on his allotment', wrote Miss Bennett. 'For transport he then used a tricycle which was propelled by hand with levers instead of by foot pedals. He brought his produce home in a basket attached to it, proceeding at a slow pace, usually with a string of traffic behind him. . .'

FOOT-AND-MOUTH FINES

14 January 1938

An outbreak of foot-and-mouth disease in the county is proving costly to some dog owners.

A foxhound belonging to Ernest Brown of Thomas Street dug its way of its run and was found by the police 'out of control' at Cliffe Corner and taken to the pound. When he went to claim the dog Mr Brown was summoned for allowing it to 'stray in a foot-and-mouth disease infected area, and fined ten shillings. A similar fine was imposed on Mrs May Cheeseman of South Street whose dog had squeezed under her back garden gate and gone for a run by itself on the golf course.

❖ ❖ ❖

VICE-CONSUL AND CAR GO INTO THE OUSE

16 September 1938

The Portuguese vice-consul, Senor Luise Rego, had a narrow escape from serious injury at 4am on Tuesday morning when he was on his way to Newhaven to meet friends off the night boat from Dieppe. The car he was driving veered to the offside at the end of South Street, mounted a raised bank, and dropped about 20ft into the river, ending up on its roof. Fortunately it was low water and Senor Rego was able to scramble out and climb up the bank. He reported the matter at the police station where he was provided with dry clothes and other assistance and returned to London by train.

CHURCH HALL IS A PRESENT TO THE PARISH

28 January 1938

Sir Frank and Lady Sanderson are providing St Michael's, Malling, with a new church hall next to the school, which is at 108-112 Malling Street. It has been designed by Wootton and Godfrey and replaces the now totally inadequate Army hut that has served the parish for many years. The building, which is of brick and stone under a tiled roof, is approached from the pavement by a path across a small lawn. Immediately inside the entrance there are cloakrooms and a kitchen with a serving counter opening on to the 40ft by 27ft main hall which has a large platform that can be folded back into a recess to give additional floor space. There are two small rooms at the far end that can be reached from the inside or from the outside of the building.

Financial threat to the future of bonfire

4 March 1938

Authority has, over the centuries, tried its best to suppress bonfire night celebrations in Lewes. The latest move in the ongoing game is a financial one. The Chief Constable, Mr R E Brefitt, has written to all the bonfire societies reminding them that under the terms of their street collection permits, all money raised in this way must go to the named charities. It has been the general practice of the societies to lump together income from all sources, including the street collections, deduct their expenses, and give the remainder to local charities

The Cliffe Bonfire Society, which resigned from the Bonfire Council in 1931 as it wished to keep up the tradition of burning an effigy of Pope Paul V, saw the letter as a threat to the future of bonfire. It suggested that the societies should get together and possibly send a deputation to the Chief Constable to discuss the matter. Last year it cost Cliffe £60 to mount its display – a sum which included the payment of £20 for two bands. Street collecting boxes had brought in £18 and a donation of £2 was made to the Victoria Hospital. In April it was arranged for a delegation to meet the Chief Constable to see if the wording of the street collection permits could be altered but what, if any, progress was made was not reported.

The celebrations of 5 November 1938 were to be the last for six years. Cliffe's tableau, in spite of Neville Chamberlain's 'peace in our time' announcement on his return from Munich in September that year, was of a huge flaming volcano, symbolising the 'Eruption of Europe'.

MUNICH CRISIS BRINGS OUT THE MASKS

September 1938

The world was waiting for war – and everyone in this country for their gas masks – when Hitler, having brought Austria into the Third Reich, turned acquisitive eyes on the Sudetenland and Czechoslovakia and precipitated the Munich crisis. The gas masks were distributed with surprising suddenness. Loud speaker vans toured the town telling residents to stay indoors from 6pm to accept delivery of the masks which had, since April, been assembled by teams of volunteers. They came in three sizes – small, medium and large. There were Mickey Mouse shaped ones for young children and for babies there were cylinders into which air was pumped by bellows.

A testing time for civil defences

December 1938 – September 1939

Government directives to local authorities on what action should be taken to protect the public from air and gas attack had been issued, and all too often ignored, since 1936 when Hitler's troops marched into the demilitarised zone of the Rhineland. Some action, however, was taken in the Cliffe. A first aid post was set up in the church hall and a room in one of the three shops awaiting demolition on Cliffe Corner was turned into an ARP demonstration centre.

The first public air raid shelters were trenches lined with concrete, steel or wood and cellars of private houses were reinforced by the council on the understanding that the householders would make them available to the public during raids. By 1940 the British Concrete Federation had produced a communal shelter made of interlocking concrete beams braced with steel sections. It was partially buried in the ground and its exposed sides and top covered with the excavated soil. Corrugated iron Anderson shelters, named after the Home Secretary Sir John Anderson, were distributed and dug into gardens of private houses and for interior use there were the Morrison shelters – steel tables under which families could crouch during raids.

It was not until after the Munich crisis that the town began to test its defences. A mock air raid was staged on 20 February 1939 during which the new siren was sounded and 'casualties' rescued from houses that were being demolished in Morris Road. In June there were trial blackouts and a 'reception of evacuees' rehearsed at the secondary school in Mountfield Road.

On 1 September the first of the 2,400 real evacuees to be sent over the next two days to the Lewes area arrived on the 9.50am train from London. The Odeon cinema was one of the centres from which they were collected by their host families or taken by billeting officers to homes that had agreed to have them.

'The reception of the evacuees represented the most remarkable feat of organisation the county has known,' reported the *Sussex Express* proudly on 8 September

Not so praiseworthy was the council's refusal to let its education sub-committee spend £2,700 on providing air raid shelters for its schools. Instead it decided to store the construction materials at a cost of £1,500. This bureaucratic blunder resulted in hurriedly-erected shelters that leaked when it rained and a fortnight's delay in reopening the schools after the summer holidays.

GOLF CLUB GOES TO WAR

17 September 1940

The eight members who attended Lewes Golf Club's annual meeting in June had the job of closing it down for the duration. They sacked the steward and stewardess, had the telephone taken away and returned the electric cooker to the firm from which it was hired. They also tried, unsuccessfully, to return the lease to the landlord. Three months later the two clubhouses were requisitioned by the Army and anti-aircraft guns set up on the course on Cliffe Hill.

SHELTER SITES
December 1941

It took the council two years to provide air raid shelters for the 12,000 people in the borough. The type, location and seating accommodation of those in the Cliffe and South Malling are:

PUBLIC SHELTERS

South Street	24
Malling Street	24
Cliffe Corner	50

SCHOOL SHELTER

South Malling	140

BCF COMMUNAL SHELTERS

Malling
front of Mill House

Mill Road	50
top of Mill Road	50
end of road to	
Malling Down	50

Cliffe
South Street

at rear of No 57	50
at rear of No 27	50
at side of Wille Cottages	25

Malling Street

rear of old rectory	50
rear of Nos 94-96	50
rear of No 5 (access	
from Chapel Hill)	50
in Coombe	50
Rear of Jireh Chapel	24

Chapel Hill
on site of demolished

house	50

BRICK SURFACE SHELTERS

Odeon car park	120
rear of 30 South Street	36

Cliffe High Street

Harvey's Brewery	48
Povey's Passage	36
Greens Passage	48
rear of No 19	48

Malling Street

rear of Caffyns	96
rear of Wharf House	96

Morris Road

at end of	48

First wartime alert is a false alarm

3 September 1939

It was 11.15am on a fine Sunday morning when the Prime Minister, Neville Chamberlain, told the nation that a state of war existed between this country and Germany. Seven minutes later the sirens sounded. An aircraft that could not be readily identified had been seen approaching the coast. It was found to be friendly and the 'All Clear' was given. There was another false alarm three days later after which the siren on Cliffe church was silent until 7 June the following year and the Battle of Britain began.

The black out was observed with meticulous care as darkness fell that night. An infringement of the Emergency Lighting Regulations could, on summary conviction, result in up to three months in prison, a fine of up to £100, or both. Next day there was a notice outside the Odeon cinema saying that it would be closed until further notice. Much to everyone's relief the 'further notice' came a week or so later when an order was made permitting 'cinemas, football grounds and other places entertainment in rural and reception areas to open until 10pm'.

People became used to taking their gas masks everywhere and quickly adjusted their daily routine to combine their normal occupations with fire watching, first-aiding and other war work. Weeks passed, then months without an air raid alert. There was little demand for the services of all those who had volunteered and the only reminders of an ever present danger were the BBC news bulletins reporting Hitler's storm troopers' remorseless progress to the Channel coast. This all changed in June 1940 when France fell.

BILLINGSGATE COMES TO THE CLIFFE

Part of the wholesale fish market at Billingsgate was moved in the first week of the war to Caffyns Garage in the Cliffe. Now fishmongers from all parts of the county turn up in their vans at 7am to collect supplies of fish which come by the lorry load, packed in ice, from Grimsby. The boxes are unloaded by 22 Billingsgate fish porters and taken to the packing station set up in the garage in Malling Streeet. Then the daily auction begins with bids of 'twelve bob (60p) a stone (6.3kg)' for hake and boxes of haddock fetching six shillings (30p) a stone.

Hit and run raiders, flying bombs and the effects of friendly fire

The skies over England were as much a battleground as any foreign field as Hitler tried to establish air supremacy prior to invading Britain. After the daytime dog fights of the Battle of Britain there was the nightly drone of German bombers on the way to drop their deadly cargo on London and to jettison their remaining bombs on Sussex as they returned to their bases in France.

4 October 1940

The blast from a bomb that exploded around 10am near the river bank at Southerham cracked the glass in the windows of Elphick's shop in Cliffe High Street.

5 October 1940

At about 9.30am the following morning raiders returning from an attack on London dropped their remaining load on Lewes. The bombs fell in a line from near the Martyrs' Memorial on Cliffe Hill to the Cockshut at Southover. One that crashed into the kitchen of Horne Lodge in Chapel Hill failed to explode and the occupants had to move in with friends and relations for a few days while it was dealt with by a bomb disposal squad.

20 January 1943

Two people were killed and eleven seriously injured when enemy planes swept over Lewes at roof top height at midday, dropping six high explosive bombs and spraying the streets with machine gun and cannon fire.

There were no casualties or damage to property in the Cliffe and South Malling as a result of this raid – but it was a near thing. That morning there had been a special showing at the Odeon of *The Young Mr Pitt* for the senior pupils of schools in the the town and a long crocodile of girls and boys was making its way back to the grammar schools and Mountfield Road Secondary School when the bombers came over. They dived into the nearest buildings for cover, emerging unscathed when the 'All Clear' sounded.

In all there were 1,051 air raid alerts, the later ones for the pilotless V1s, nicknamed 'doodlebugs' on their way to London.

In the last years of the war, friendly fire did almost as much damage as the Luftwaffe.

On **14 April 1944** Harold Snaith received head injuries when a smoke mortar went through the roof of a cowshed at Ranscombe Farm; on **20 January 1945** a 3- inch shell was found by the road 50 yards from the Prince of Wales pub; and in **July 1945** twenty RAF cannon shells smashed through the windows of 28 Malling Street, a house two doors away from the Dorset Arms.

FILM FANS BREAK THE RULES

From June 1940 Lewes was part of a prohibited area and only residents and those with a genuine reason to be there were allowed in. Identity cards had to be shown at checkpoints in South Street and Malling Street and there were frequent spot checks by the police within the area. It was in one of these checks at the Odeon cinema on a Sunday, that two film fans from Uckfield were found. Their excuse that the Uckfield cinema was not open on Sunday was not appreciated by the court and they were each fined five shillings.

TANK TAKES A FATAL TURN

21 March 1941

A skid by a 26 ton tank named Rapscallion as it turned from Cliffe High Street into South Street, had fatal consequences. It slewed round, hit a parked van and crashed into a shed in Rusbridge's yard where boot and shoe repairer 52 year old Alfred Humphreys was serving a customer, Mrs Annie Buckwell. She sustained serious leg injuries, but Humphrey, an air raid warden at the Cliffe Corner post, was found dead on arrival at Victoria Hospital.

The tank, driven by Trooper James Webber of the 44th Royal Tank Regiment, was one of five on their way from Stanmer Park to the training ground at Seaford Head. They had negotiated Cliffe bridge safely and four turned right into South Street without trouble. An inquest jury exonerated Trooper Webber from all blame for the accident.

WINDOW SHOPPING?

A Bren gun carrier lost its grip on the road when crossing Cliffe Bridge and ended up among the toys, games and carnival goods in the windows of Cliffe Bazaar at 4a Cliffe High Street.

The street lights come on again . . .

September 1944

From the launching of the Second Front with the D-Day landings of 6 June conditions on the Home Front began to improve. One of the first inconveniences to go was the blackout. Not that the lights came on all over the town on 27 September – only from 10pm to midnight – and only one third of the lamps were alight. Full street lighting was not restored until July the following year.

VE Day was 8 May 1945 and fires blazed on Cliffe Hill as some members of the Home Guard disposed of a quantity of surplus anti-tank Fougasse drums containing a mixture of paraffin and engine oil. There was a more organised fire display the next day. A combined bonfire societies procession of 2,000 torches, led by band of Lewes Air Training Corps, started at 9.15pm from the Swan in Southover, went all round the town and finally along Cliffe High Street and up School Hill to the war memorial where an effigy of Hitler was burned.

The process of dismantling the town's defences then began. The 'restricted to military use only' Bailey bridge which spanned the river from Soap Factory Lane to Eastgate Street was taken away and the golf course and its buildings handed back to the council. Dismantling the civil defences took longer. Some air raid shelters in gardens backing on to the western slopes of Cliffe Hill remain to this day and although the 5,000 gallon static water tank has gone from Cliffe Corner the car park there is still edged with anti-tank concrete 'sharks' teeth'.

Food rationing did not end with the war. It was extended to bread in July 1946 and potatoes in November 1949. However clothes came off coupons in May that year – and soap and petrol in 1950.

6. A HALF CENTURY OF DEVELOPMENT PLUS A HURRICANE AND TWO FLOODS

1951-2002

In the last half of the twentieth century the Cliffe lost its cinema, its burial ground, its cement works, a cluster of little streets by the Great Sewer and most of its food and general shops. Multiples like the Maypole, the International, the Home and Colonial closed down; so did the post office; the butchers; the fishmongers and Timothy Whites, the chemists. In their place came antiques shops and centres and businesses geared to the leisure and tourist trade.

Where the inner relief road and the proposed bypass were to go kept the planners arguing – and traders and residents worrying – until the question was finally settled in the 1970s.

It was getting daily more difficult for buses, large lorries and an ever-increasing number of cars to get up and down Cliffe High Street. And on summer Sunday evenings traffic in South Street and Malling Street would be at a standstill as carloads of visitors to the coast headed back to their homes inland and fruit lorries from the Continent, banned by weight from using Newhaven bridge, tried to make their way to the markets of London. This situation was slightly eased in 1969 when the Ouse was bridged by Phoenix Causeway, connecting Eastgate with Soap Factory Lane as the wartime Bailey bridge had done. It was then a question, as far as the residents of the Cliffe were concerned, of deciding on the best way to link up with the southern bypass – either by tunnelling under the hill from behind the Snowdrop to the north of Cuilfail or doubling the width of South Street by demolishing houses on the river side. In the end the tunnellers won, thanks to the invention of new cutting machinery and the gov-ernment's introduction of compensation payments for homeowners affected by traffic schemes.

It was very different at Malling. The council and private developers met little opposition when they set about transforming the area from a community with a population numbered in hundreds to one of many thousands. They started on land north of Spences Lane, uncovering a Roman road when digging the foundations for a block of flats at the Martlets. After the closure of the railway line to Uckfield, houses, bungalows and flats for more than 2,000 people were built on thirty three acres of farmland to the north of the church. The new residents of New Malling had splendid views from their country estate but a long walk to the shops. However, their situation was slightly eased by the expansion of the Brooks Road industrial estate, the construction of a link road from Church Lane to Brooks Road and the opening of Tesco's superstore with its car park and petrol station on the river bank to the north of Phoenix Causeway.

There were proposals of a different sort for land around Malling Deanery and on Malling Down. The former was designated a conservation area and the forty-five acres of Malling Down, including the combe known because of its contours as Fat Belly Woman, became a nature reserve. However, this half century is likely to be remembered more for what the weather did rather than what was built and where. The floods of October 1960 and in September 2000 made hundreds homeless and the hurricane of October 1987 left a trail of damage across the whole south-east.

CRICKET BAT MAKER

Nick Cochrane at work on the upper floor of the old barn adjoining the garage at 66 South Street, where he opened a cricket bat factory in 1951.

Golfers are back on course

April 1953

The council has handed back the leases of the golf course and its club houses on Cliffe Hill to the Lewes Golf Club, together with grants to make up for any losses.

It had agreed to take them over in 1945 when the club had only a handful of members. It has since received £5,132 12s 9d (£5,132.63p) from the Compensation Fund for removing scars of wartime from the course and its clubhouses. Soil excavated from the housing project at Landport was brought by the lorry load up Chapel Hill and used to fill in the trenches and wartime gun emplacements, and the council also made improvements to the course, and built a reservoir to provide it with a water supply.

The decision to give the golf club back to its members rather than to run it as a municipal course was possibly influenced by the fact that the maintenance and administration costs were £1,000 a year.

Rectory is now 'the house with the caravan'

1954

The Georgian house bought as a rectory for the parish in 1930 and occupied by only one incumbent and only for seven years, no longer belongs to the diocese. Brantwood, 21 Malling Street has been sold to Mr and Mrs Joseph Light who have moved from Hastings with sons Joe, Jerry, John and Jimmy and daughter, Eileen.

'We had relatives already living here', recalled Eileen, now Mrs Bradbury and living in Mill Road. 'My grandfather and two uncles were in Spences Lane and my cousin, John, had the scrapyard at Southerham.'

When Seeboard moved out of the nearby White Swan, which it had used as a store for many years, her brother Joe opened an antiques business there and bought a gipsy caravan as part of the stock. He parked it, temporarily, as he thought, in the drive of Brantwood, and it became one of the things to see in the Cliffe.

'My mother took it over as her garden room and people would often stop for a chat whenever they saw her sitting under the canopy in the front of it,' said Eileen. Joe was not able to sell the caravan but he did make a discovery which provided him with something unusual for his shop. Buried beneath the silt that almost filled the cellars under rooms at the front of the old inn he found hundreds of coloured glass nightlight holders that may well have been used for the festive illuminations that marked the silver jubilee of King George V in 1936.

Roman road found on site of new flats at Malling

1953

Council workmen began digging the foundations for a block of flats at the Martletts and in doing so found a Roman road running parallel to Church Lane. Lying on the flint surface was a 5ft 8in-skeleton and beside it was a knife and an iron ring. Several feet away, in a ditch beside the road, was another skeleton and a gilt bronze saucer-shaped brooch.

Further along the road to the west a group of Romano-British cremation burials was discovered. Among the funerary jars was a Samian ware dish with MM⌐ scratched on its side and in the ashes in another jar were a dozen or so iron hob-nails – an indication, perhaps, that the occupant died with his boots on.

Two years later, when the ground was being levelled for a playing field for the new Church of England mixed school on the corner of Malling Hill and Church Lane, two skeletons, probably Saxon, were found buried above the same Roman road.

The new school, which cost £9,701 to build, replaces the cramped premises of the old parochial school at 108 Malling Street, next to the garage. When it opened in 1956 it had 100 pupils in its light and airy classrooms. By the 1970s, when families had settled in to the bungalows, houses and blocks of flats of New Malling, it had more than 250.

At Southerham, in the 1970s, the farmhouse and its barns and other buildings were converted to holiday homes.

BAD YEARS FOR BONFIRE
1950s

The survival of South Street Juvenile bonfire society, formed in 1913, was in doubt in the early 1950s. Adult membership, or rather the lack of it, was the main problem. When the society reformed after the war 250 children and 50 adults had enrolled but by the mid-1950s numbers had declined drastically for the society's youngsters, as they grew up, were going on to join the ranks of the town's adult societies. In 1955 it looked as if there would be no celebrations on the Fifth but there was a last minute revival of interest, five processions were arranged and South Street Juveniles were invited to lead the United Procession.

NOWHERE TO PLAY
18 March 1955

Malling Cricket Club has everything it needs for success – except a pitch to play on. Last season it played eight away matches, winning one. The secretary, Charles Painter, told the three members who were at the annual meeting, that he had written to the council about the Stanley Turner ground.

Floods wash out Fifth celebrations

3 November 1960

More than 8 inches of rain fell in October, a month when the average rainfall over the previous ten years had been 2.78 inches. The ground was waterlogged and the steady downpours of the last few days produced too much surface water for the tidal Ouse to carry away to the sea.

First to flood was the Winterbourne Stream. It could not empty the waters that had drained down from the heights above Kingston into the swollen river. Instead, it burst its banks and flooded the station, the cattle market and houses in and around Grange Road.

At the next high tide, on Thursday evening, the Ouse rose by 3ft and flooded parts of Malling Street, Cliffe High Street, Morris Road and South Street. The water rose above the window sills of the new houses in Orchard Road. Thomas Street flooded to a depth of 4ft and Miss B M Page and her sister had to be rescued from the upper windows of No 10. There was 2ft of water in the back of the off-licence in Malling Street and it seeped through and covered the floor of the shop.

Victor Value's in Cliffe High Street was swimming in porridge as packages of oats fell to the floor. The oats were followed by packets of soap powder which turned to foam and oozed under the door and out into the street. In the Odeon car park tons of coke stacked in a corner were washed around by the floodwater. When it drained away the car park was found to be neatly resurfaced with nubs of coke.

Furniture dealer, Fred Arnold, found a goldfish swimming around in his flooded front room in Morris Road. He took it to Mrs Bennett at No 18 and her daughter, Elizabeth, put it in the pond in their garden.

The levels from Malling to Hamsey were totally submerged and those to the south were under water as far as Beddingham. In addition to riverside business premises some 620 houses were flooded and total damage was said to be in excess of £300,000.

Lewes Bonfire Council decided it would be irresponsible to bring large crowds into an area were streets were still under water and cancelled the celebrations set for Satruday. Some of the societies would not have been able to put on much of a show. Members of South Street Juveniles found their torch shed up to its roof in water but the tableau, stored on higher ground, not too badly damaged. A fortnight later, with torches re-rolled and tableau repaired, they had a bonfire in the chalkpit, burnt effigies of Robert Catesby and Guy Fawkes, and took a collection for the Flood Relief Fund.

An Eastwood cement works lorry makes its wet way along Cliffe High Street on Friday morning.
Photo: Sussex Express

House with a ghost of a man in a white coat

1963

Ranscombe Villa, a four bedroom house on the south side of Ranscombe Hill on the road to Eastbourne, was built in 1921 by the Lewes Portland Cement Company for its manager, John Stone. He was struck by lightning when planting some fruit trees in the garden that surrounded the house and died. Has he, perhaps, stayed on in spirit to watch his trees grow?

When Judy and Christopher Moore bought the house several months ago they were told about the haunting by a previous tenant – coincidentally someone sent by Curtis and Co to advise them about a new pump for the well. When living there the hydraulics engineer and his children had often seen the figure of a man in a white coat – sometimes in the house but more often in the garden – but his wife had not.

The Moores noticed that when their three dogs were in the vicinity of the air raid shelter that had been built into the slope by the steps leading up to the road they would go to the point as if they could see something their owners could not. More, and stranger, confirmation came from Christopher's aunt, Mrs Lilian Wackett, who was a medium.

On her first visit to the house she said she was aware of a presence.

'Who is it?' asked her nephew.

'His name is John Stone,' she replied.

Judy's mother, Mrs Elsie Morris, also saw the man in the white coat – as a clear, sharp figure and not as a ghostly apparition. On one occasion she walked from the back garden to the south facing front of the house and was amazed to see her son-in-law, wearing a white overall, painting a garden seat.

'How did you get past me?' she asked. 'I clearly saw you by that old air raid shelter under the road only a moment ago.'

NOTE: The house was demolished in 1972 as part of the scheme for a bypass to the south of Lewes.

CHANGE OF PLAN CLOSES POST OFFICE **4 September 1964**	Yet another change of plan in respect of the Lewes Relief Road scheme has caused the closure of the only post office in the parish of South Malling. East Sussex Country Council has compulsorily purchased 69 Malling Street and intends to demolish it to make way for the new road. Miss May Godden, postmistress there for the past twenty-one years, has resigned rather than wait to be given notice to quit. The nearest post office for the residents of Malling will be at 49 Cliffe High Street in the radio and cycle shop a few doors away from F W Woolworth and Co.

ART FIND
1967

An eighteenth-century, four-panel Chinese lacquer screen depicting a lion hunt has been found behind layers of wallpaper in a house in Chapel Hill. It forms part of the left wall of the entrance hall of Lamb House where June Welton and her sister, Beryl, do bed and breakfast and afternoon teas.

Pages from the *Lewes Journal* form the first layer covering the screen. They date from 1794-96 when the house was used as a store by Thomas Baldy, creator of the Hanging Gardens and proprietor of the china shop next door.

LAST ORDERS
1969

Two more old inns have closed, both of them in South Street. The Fountain and the Thatched House began their licensed lives as beerhouses in the late eighteenth century. They each, at times, played host to the parish's vestry meetings and its bonfire societies.

The Fountain, where Mrs Elsie Brooker pulled pints for nearly 40 years, is now a private house. The Thatched House, built in 1803 in front of the House of Industry, is being demolished and a terrace of Regency style houses will be built on the site.

New footbridge links Malling to Lewes
February 1965

The old Deanery suspension bridge has been replaced by a sturdier and steadier structure. It was formally opened today by the mayor, Cllr A C Barber, and named Willey's Bridge after Cllr Len Willey, the Bridge Ward representative who campaigned so strenuously for it to be built.

The number of people needing to cross the river to their place of work increased considerably with the post-war development of New Malling. They had no right of access to the private Deanery bridge, so the alternative was for them to go along Spences Lane to Malling Street, up Cliffe High Street and over the road bridge.

There has been a footbridge from the Deanery to the Pells since the eighteenth century, its name changing with successive owners. A three-span black tarred wooden structure with a pier on either bank, known as Admiral Currey's bridge, was replaced in 1935 by Sir Frank Sanderson MP with the present single span white painted iron suspension bridge with tall iron towers for its chains.

Who could or could not use these private bridges has depended, throughout the centuries, on the owner of Malling Deanery. It was a privilege that could be withdrawn at any time – as it was, so the story goes, when Robert Lamdin was living there. He gave a party, at which drinks were served, to welcome a vicar to the parish. However, the new incumbent was a total abstainer and expressed his disapproval of the alcoholic hospitality offered. His host responded by keeping the bridge gate locked on Sundays, so denying Lewes members of his congregation – except for a chosen few – a short cut to the church.

Ancient graveyard had to go

August 1972

The disused graveyard on the east side of Malling Street was screened off from the road while it is cleared of the 150 graves it contained. It had to go to make way for the new lay-out of the county council's inner relief road the first phase of which was completed with the opening of Phoenix Causeway in 1969.

St Thomas's church never had a churchyard. It was surrounded by the Fair Place, where, from 1421, chartered fairs were held twice a year and a market every Wednesday. The 'ancient burying place' of the parish was said by Horsfield to be 'on the east side of North Street under the overhanging cliff'. It was enlarged twice in the eighteenth century and was extended in 1846 over the parish boundary into Malling (see pages 36 and 80).

A transcript has been made of the inscriptions on the gravestones, which date from 1764 to 1866, and they have been piled into two arched entrances on the Cliffe Hill side of the site – perhaps the remains of the 'two houses on the south side' bought for £28 in 1796 – and cemented over.

In one unmarked grave fifteen skeletons were found, no doubt the victims of one of the smallpox epidemics of the eighteen century when the graveyard was twice enlarged. They have been re-interred in Lewes cemetery.

NOTE: The site is marked today by an undated plaque, on the wall of the northern entrance to the tunnel.

The broken up gravestones in their last resting place in archways under the cliff, now covered by the north east entrance wall of the tunnel. Photo: Zena Rector.

TRAIN COMES OFF THE RAILS

15 June 1976

The 6.44pm passenger train to Ore was travelling at 35-40mph across Southerham junction when the points were moved under the second coach and the last three carriages came off the rails.

Five passengers were taken to hospital suffering from shock and the guard had slight injuries to his back and ribs. Worst affected was the signalman on duty in the nearby box. He collapsed when being interviewed after the accident and spent the night in hospital.

An inquiry decided the de-railment was an 'isolated case of a signalman disregarding well-understood rules in respect of the use of the release key on the electrical and mechanical locking of points and signals'.

A CLUB FOR ALL SORTS – AND SOME SPORTS
1970

A hall that can seat 125, with a licensed bar and lounge, has been built at the west end of Spences Lane with cash from council and money raised by local residents. It houses the Malling Community Centre's senior citizens' club, children's play group, mother and toddlers group, youth club and disco dance group together with the Bridge View Social Club which has four pool teams, ladies and mixed darts teams and a quiz team.

'THE END' AT THE ODEON
2 October 1971

The cinema which was a major entertainment centre for the area during the war has shown its last film. The national anthem was played at the Odeon for the last time on Saturday night after the screening of *Two Mules for Sister Sarah.*, a Western starring Clint Eastwood and Shirley MacLaine. The increasing popularity of television, particularly since the introduction of colour in 1967, has resulted in fewer and fewer people leaving their own firesides to visit the cinema in Cliffe High Street.

CENTENARY
1979

James Chandler came to Lewes from Broughton Astley in Leicestershire and set up as a coal merchant in 1879. He expanded into the merchanting of bricks and other building materials and in 1948 the firm he founded, James Chandler (Lewes) Ltd., moved on to the former gas works site by the river.

At long last – a bypass

August 1975

Work has started on a £4.9 million bypass that will take the A27 traffic to the south of Lewes and away from the narrow streets through the centre of the town and the Cliffe. It will be a 2½-mile long, four-lane highway and run from Hope in the Valley to the west to a new roundabout at Southerham.

Lewes has been trying for 148 years to get a bypass. In 1827 the borough council planned to run a road from Malling Hill across the Brooks and over a bridge at the Pells into North Street. This scheme was collapsed when Cliffe traders, fearing loss of custom, widened their narrow High Street by 9ft. In 1924-25 it was the county council that suggested a bypass, again across Malling Brooks, but backed down in face of fierce opposition and widened Cliffe bridge instead.

In the plan it published in 1953 East Susssex County Council proposed an inner relief road that would involve the demolition of some 150 old houses and virtually cut the town in two. Almost everyone was against it so an independent report was commissioned and it came down in favour of a southern bypass.

However, when the Ministry of Transport's route for this bypass was published in 1971, there were more howls of protest for it showed a road running on a viaduct across Winterbourne to join the A275 at the prison crossroads. A public inquiry upheld the plan but Winterbourne residents, not wanting cars thundering past their homes at bedroom window level, did not give up. They persisted with their protest and in 1974 the Department of the Environment gave in and scrapped the link road scheme.

After a century and a half of hassle all went well with the construction of the cuttings, embankments and bridges of the new road. The long, hot summer of 1976 gave the 170 men then employed on the site ideal conditions for the work and the bypass was completed two months ahead of schedule.

Thousands walk through £3 million tunnel

30 November 1980

A rotating cutter head mounted on a specially modified excavator was used to tunnel north-south under Cliffe Hill.
Photo: Sussex Express

This was a Sunday to remember for the thousands who took a once-in-a-lifetime walk through Cuilfail tunnel before it was officially opened on Monday.

Everyone appeared to be in party mood. They had their dogs, their babies, their bicycles and their cameras with them as they strolled up and down the 420m-long, 7.3m-wide road through the chalk, pointing out to each other where the emergency telephones were and how the electric lighting was graded so their eyes would adjust as they went from the natural daylight to near darkness at the centre.

The walk through, from 2pm to 4pm, was from the southern end only. And it was at the southern end, the next day, that the tunnel was formally declared open by the county council's Highways and Works Committee chairman, Peter Gladwin. He then handed a pair of scissors to South Street campaigner, Rosalind Barrie, and she cut the ribbon draped across the entrance to allow his official car, with him in it, to be the first vehicle to go through.

The first tame rabbit to travel through the tunnel did so later in the day. He was three-year-old Belgian hare called Digby and he belonged to schoolmaster David Sykes and his wife, Anne, who were then living in Wallands. They made the journey purposely to give Digby a claim to fame. South Street residents, delighted to be living in a cul-de-sac instead of a trunk road, had a celebratory lunch in the church hall on the following Sunday.

The tunnel was to have opened in May this year but there were problems with subsidence and three houses on Cuilfail, in which serious cracks appeared, were bought by the government. An eight day strike by the miners, worried about end-of-the-job payments, also held up the work.

PHOENIX CENTRE OPENS
1980

The Phoenix Centre, a single-storey building at the north end of North Court, is now open. In the jargon of the day it is 'a multi-purpose centre to meet the social, creative, rehabilitative and the therapeutic needs of the elderly, the physically handicapped, single parents with children, the mentally disturbed, those recovering from addiction, social isolation and loneliness'.

In plain English it is a pleasant place for people with problems to meet, get help, have their hair done, their feet attended to or settle down for a cup of tea and a chat.

❖ ❖ ❖

ALL THE YEAR ROUND WATER
1983

The reservoir behind the fourteenth green on the golf course, which supplies the Cuilfail estate and the club, has often run dry in the summer. Now Southern Water has spent £73,000 on overhauling the system and installing new mains and boosters to lift the water up hill.

ROCK FALL SHUTS TUNNEL
1 March 1985

Cuilfail tunnel was closed from Friday to Sunday because rocks, loosened by a sudden thaw, were falling on to the roadway at the southern end. Scaffolding and netting have been put up against the cliff, which is owned by the Department of Transport, and a full survey is to be made.

CHAPEL IS UNSAFE
1986

The Jireh chapel, the only Grade I listed building in Lewes, has woodworm, wet rot and beetle. It has been declared unsafe and its congregation of Calvinistic Independents have had to move out and worship elsewhere.

Fifty jobs to go when cement works close

4 May 1981

close in July with the loss of fifty jobs. The Rugby Portland Cement Company said that the plant, where cement has been manufactured since 1902, is uneconomic in the present recession. The kiln on the site has been working non-stop since 1928 and cement from it was used to make the sectional Mulberry harbours of the D-Day landings.

Since the Lewes Portland Cement Company began operations in the Snowdrop and Southerham chalk pits in 1902, clay has been brought up by barge from Denton and lifted by crane on to

waiting trucks that were hauled to the kiln by by a succession of small locomotives. Pictured left is *Atlas, No 17* a Hawthorn Leslie 0-4-0ST. It was replaced in 1966 by the diesel locomotive made by the Drewry Car Company which is still being used for shifting cement about the plant. Rugby Portland Cement is keeping part of the site as a depot and the rest is to be developed as an industrial estate.

An island site for Brian the Snail

25 September 1983

A 2.7m high mathematical spiral in Portland stone, 'reflecting the form of an ammonite', has been placed on the traffic island on the Malling side of the tunnel.

Brian the Snail, as it was immediately named after a character in the children's TV programme *Magic Roundabout,* was carved from seven blocks of Portland stone by sculptor Peter Randall-Page, who has exhibited in Nottingham, Liverpool, Bristol and London.

It was commissioned by the county council, cost £12,000, and was paid for jointly by South Eastern Arts and the contractors, Mountfield Roadstone. Ammonites are among many fossilised marine creatures found in Sussex downland chalk of the Jurassic to Upper Cretaceous geological periods.

The cement works in South Street are to

Peter Randall Page (left), and his assistant, remove the lugs which held the chains on which the sculpture was lowered on to its plinth. Photo: Sussex Express

END OF THE ODEON
1982

The Odeon cinema, closed since 1971, has become a visual embarrassment to shoppers and shopkeepers in the Cliffe. 'Repair it and reopen it' was the majority verdict of the survey conducted by Lewes Young Conservatives two years ago and last year a petition with 3,500 signatures was sent to the district council by Cliffe Traders demanding some action be taken about the eyesore. Demolition work has now started on the Art Deco facade and an arcade of shops is to be built on the site.

PUB WITH A PIG IS SOLD
14 November 1986

The Manxman in Malling Street, a free house owned by Mike Davies, has been sold to Harvery's Brewery. It will revert to its original name of the Dorset Arms and future patrons will not be sharing the bars with the Manxman's animal attractions – the landlord's pet pig called Truffles and his tame rat which ran around the bar counter.

❖ ❖ ❖

Orchids are back on Malling Down

1985-2000

A nature reserve has been established by Sussex Wildlife Trust on Malling Down. Its steep slopes were, until the war, grazed by sleep and cattle and downland flowers including orchids, gentians, dropwort and rampion, grew there in profusion. However, with the changes in farming practice brought about by this country joining the EEC, nature's four-legged lawnmowers were moved away, much of the grassland became overgrown with brambles and brush-wood, and rubbish and rotting vegetation piled up in the disused chalkpits beside the Ringmer road.

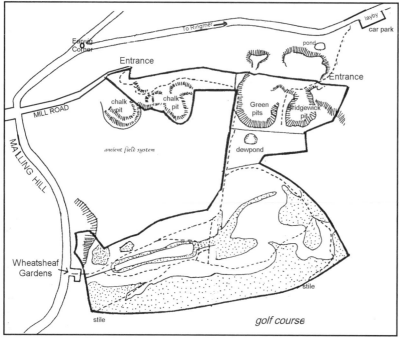

Malling Down nature reserve is within the outlined area.

A decade or so later. it is all very different The scrub has been cleared, a dewpond built on the top of the hill to supply water to a couple of cattle troughs, fences have been repaired and replaced and livestock is back grazing the grassland.

The reserve is always open. There are three entrances to it – from Wheatsheaf Gardens, from the end of Mill Road and from the Ringmer road where there is car parking in the layby. The best place to find orchids and other specialised downland flowers is in the Green Pits and the best time is from May to August. On warm summer nights the grassy banks are spattered with points of light as glow worms hunt for their supper of snails. In daylight there are many thousands of spotted orchids, and thirty species of butterfly, among them the rare Adonis Blue whose caterpillars thrive on the horseshoe and kidney vetches which grows on the reserve.

Spotted orchid   *The Adonis Blue*   *The kidney vetch*

The Tower of London is a much admired regular runner in the annual raft race on the Ouse to Newhaven which, since its inception in 1972, has raised many thousands of pounds for charity. It was started by members of Lewes Rowing Club and in 1975, when it had grown beyond their organisational resources, it was taken over by the Hailsham Round Table.
Photo: Sussex Express.

Hurricane causes havoc in the south-east

16 October 1987

South-westerly winds gusting up to 85mph raged over south east England for four hours from 1am. Millions of trees were uprooted, lorries and cars overturned, caravans wrecked, slates came crashing down from roofs, power supplies were disrupted and 3,000 miles of telephone lines torn down.

After a night of howling wind, bangs, thuds and the sound of breaking glass as shop blinds were torn off, chimneys blown down, and garden sheds uprooted, it quietened down around dawn. It was then a matter of coping without electricity and, in many cases, a telephone; assessing the damage; and getting someone to repair it.

Houses and shops in part of Malling Street had to be evacuated while troops used high explosive to clear fallen trees from the slopes of Undercliffe. Sections of the path which is the only access to the Victorian Gothic style house with its Saxon-Rhenish tower had been swept away in the storm and Dr Janet Collett and her nine year old son Ben had to scramble up the steep slope to get home. In all some six tons of timber was winched down and loaded on to waiting lorries.

The after-the-storm scene at Lewes Rowing Club. Some of the corrugated iron sheets may well be from buildings on the golf course on top of the hill.

Finds before flats in the Fair Place

1988

Under way in Malling is a self build development of sixteen two-bedroom terraced and semi-detached houses. A self build association has been formed and its members save money by operating as a building company and being its work force. They are hard at work – usually in the evenings and at weekends – on the site which is between the council flats of Gibson's Court and the private development of Cranmer Close. When completed the houses are expected to sell for £26,000, each producing a profit of around £9,000.

Agricultural machinery retailer, Curtis and Company, which has been trading in Cliffe High Street since the early years of the nineteenth century, has moved to the new Malling industrial estate north of Phoenix Causeway. Going up in its place on the site by the church is a courtyard complex of forty-six sheltered flats and six town houses, to be known as St Thomas's Court, and a new church hall.

Before the builders

Cars, vans, even a boat used to be parked in the yard leading up to the old church hall.

moved on to the site David Rudling and students from the Institute of Archaeology did. Their excavations turned up what was to be expected from land on which fairs and stock markets had been held since the fifteenth century. Among the animal and fish bones, old clay pipes, oyster shells, lead tokens and post medieval glass and pottery in the two rubbish pits behind the church hall were fragments of two straight-sided stoneware tankards, one with the ale mark of William III and inscribed:

Thos Ford at ye King . . . . .en
In the Clift 1715

The name of the same tavern, but less of it − . . .g & Quee. . . 1715 – was on the other. The King and Queen (see page 44) was only a short walk away. Perhaps its patrons were in the habit of taking pots of ale with them to a fair and not returning the empties.

The new Cliffe industrial estate that has been developed on the site of the Rugby Portland Cement Works at the southern end of South Street.

Blowtorch starts a fire at police headquarters

4 October 1990

Black smoke pours from the roof of Malling House as firemen fight to control the blaze. Photo: Paddy Rea.

A workman's blow torch was blamed for starting the fire that swept through Malling House on Wednesday morning. At its height flames shot 20ft into the air and were only a few feet away from office of the Chief Constable, Roger Birch, who was on holiday in Portugal.

Seventy firemen with fourteen appliances managed to confine the outbreak to the southern third of the mansion built $c1720$ by John Spence, but a quarter of the roof was destroyed and much of the interior gutted. However, by February the following year it had been restored at the cost of £1 million. Sufficient Sussex oak had been found to replace the burnt roof timbers and thousands of the old peg tiles had been rescued and replaced.

Malling House became the headquarters of the East Sussex Constabulary in 1968 when the five police forces of Brighton, Eastbourne, Hastings, Hove and Rye amalgamated. The property, together with thirteen acres of land, had been sold to the county council in 1948 by Sir George Boughey who had bought it in 1924 as his country house. His London home, since leaving the Indian Civil Service in 1916, was 25 Lowndes Square.

Childhood days at Malling are described by his daughter, Hermia – Hermia Priestley a wartime GI bride now living in America – in *John Boughey, A Memoir,* an appreciation of her brother, a Rupert Brooke style cricketer and poet who was killed in action at sea in August 1940 at the age of twenty-one. Of returning there in school holidays she writes:

> Pushing open the heavy front door we were inside the hall, looking swiftly about us to make certain that everything was really the same as when we had left it . . . the stone fireplace, the floor with its black and white marble squares, my mother's red lacquer writing desk glowing against the sombre panelling; flowers, books and pictures, and the sun striking through the long staircase window . . .

TEA KETTLE ALLEY IS RE-SURFACED
October 1991

The surface of Foundry Lane, known in the nineteenth century as Tea Kettle Alley because of the big brass kettle that hung outside the iron foundry's showrooms at its entrance, has been restored to its original state of cobbles and granite cart runs.

PEDESTRIAN PRECINCT

1987

A £1½ million scheme by Lowfield Commercial Estates has turned the road running from the west of Cliffe bridge to the bottom of School Hill into a shopping precinct. complete with seats and some ornamental trees.

SHELTERED FLATS PLAN

1988

Planning approval has been given for the Sunday School adjoining the Jireh chapel to be replaced by a block of eleven retirement flats. The chapel itself, which lost a lot of its roof in last autumn's storm, is currently being restored by English Heritage at a cost of £350,000

A SURGERY ON THE RIVERSIDE

1988

The practice founded in the 1930s by Dr Joe Nicholl and Dr Sinclair in partnership with Dr Hugh Rice of Ringmer has moved from Castle Lodge, Lewes, to River Lodge, a purpose-built surgery on the site of the former children's playground on the banks of the Ouse.

The reordered interior of St Michael the Archangel with the altar and lectern at the west end. On the shiny new floor are some brightly coloured toys for children to push or ride around on.

Church is turned round to be multi-functional

18 January 1990

The completion of the first stage of re-ordering Malling parish church, built in 1628 on the foundations of the one demolished at the Dissolution, was marked on Sunday by a service of rededication conducted by the Bishop of Lewes, the Right Reverend Peter Ball. It was followed by a celebratory lunch in the much-altered interior.

Plans to enlarge the church and give it a more multi-functional role by moving the altar to the west end and building a gallery at the east end were made during the tenure of the Reverend Malcolm Colmer, vicar from 1979 to 1986. His charismatic ministry had attracted many new members to the church, the majority of them young families from New Malling. For them the church hall, built in 1938 in Malling Street, was too long a walk away. It was therefore sold to help finance the alterations which so far have cost £100,000 and taken six months to complete.

While work on replacing the original floor was in progress the lead coffins of Dr Richard Russell (see pages 38 and 41) and other parishioners from the far past were found in brick vaults beneath it. They were not disturbed.

Cliffe concerned about losing its loos

2 May 1998

The public lavatories that were built on the south-west of Cliffe Corner in 1932 have been converted to a community coffee bar with Lottery grant money and cash help from the district and parish councils. Lewes District Council has given £6,550 and leased the loos, the lottery has given £32,250 and Lewes town council £6,600.

The Nutty Wizard, as the cafe is called, is to be open from 7pm to 10.30pm on Fridays, 2pm to 5pm and 7pm to10.30pm on Saturdays and from 2pm to 5pm on Sundays.

When news leaked out two months ago of the council's plans to demolish the loos, Cliffe residents and traders were not pleased. A government inspector, at an inquiry into a another matter, said: 'To the south a modestly charged car park (Phoenix) gives access to public toilets at present in Cliffe High Street but scheduled in due course to be located into the car park'.

NOTE: As at March 2003 there are no public lavatories in the Phoenix car park or anywhere else in the Cliffe. The Nutty Wizard cafe is rarely open.

Cigarette starts a fire in four shops

26 July 1996

Fire swept through four shops in Cliffe High Street in the early hours of Friday morning. The alarm was raised by Alan Parsons, an off-duty fireman living in a flat in the street and soon more than 100 firemen, with fourteen appliances were fighting the blaze.

The fire, started by a lighted cigarette that had thrown on to bags of rubbish put outside Intersport for the refuse collection, spread quickly to Harvey's brewery shop, the Friday-Ad shop and Granada TV.

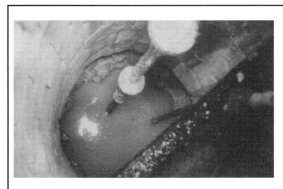

WELL FOUND

1995

Council workmen have uncovered a 6ft diameter well in Chapel Hill. It is the one that, from 1804, supplied water to the public pump outside St Thomas's church. The shaft of the well is lined with curved granite blocks and its plumbing is fairly intact. It is to be capped off at road level with a circular metal plate.

IAN PAISLEY'S CHURCH TAKES OVER JIREH CHAPEL
1 May 1998

The Free Presbyterian Church, whose Moderator is the Reverend Ian Paisley, has taken over the Jireh Chapel from the Independent Calvinists who built it in 1805. Today Dr Paisley preached at its first Free Presbyterian service to a congregation of some 400 – considerably more than the half dozen or so who returned to worship there in 1996 after the Grade 1 listed building, which had been declared unsafe eleven years previously, had been restored.

Jim North, minister for the past fifteen years, has been replaced by Noel Shields, aged thirty-seven, from Northern Ireland, a married man with four children.

RUSSIAN ICONS IN CLIFFE CHURCH
June 1996

Members of the Russian Orthodox parish of the Nativity in the Diocese of Sourozhn are going to hold their Sunday services in Cliffe church. Previously they were at Spithurst, near Barcombe, but the church there has been declared redundant and closed. All necessary permissions have been obtained from the Diocese of Chichester by the Reverend Barry Keaton, rector of St Thomas Becket church. After sung Eucharist on Sunday mornings icons will be set up in the church and Father Sergei Hackel will conduct the Russian Orthodox services there. He is at Sussex University and the majority of the members of his congregation are at colleges and higher education establishments in Brighton.

English Passage.

Rights of passage are restored
13 August 1999

English Passage has become a cul-de-sac again, no doubt to the delight of its householders. For the past thirty years the narrow pathway between the cottages and their gardens has been used as a through route from Cliffe High Street to the Phoenix Centre and the river bank. It has been replaced as a throughway by a widened and re-paved North Court which is linked to the river bank with a new path round the Riverside surgery.

This barn, which once housed a cricket bat factory, was demolished in 1998 as were the rest of the buildings on the Lewes Service Station site in South Street. They will be replaced by a development of four houses and a maisonette.

Forty years on – and yet another flood

12 October 2000

The floodwaters on their way to the sea at around 2.30pm on Thursday.
Photo: Evening Argus.

A long spell of heavy rain brought water draining off the downs into Ouse on Thursday to combine with a high spring tide and flood the low-lying areas of Cliffe and South Malling. In a matter of minutes water poured over the bank behind the new wall of Harvey's brewery and swirled across into North Court. It covered the car parks and flooded into Cliffe High Street where, at about 1.30pm, shopkeepers were still filling sandbags, brought in from Chandlers at Ringmer. By 2.30pm they were helping each other get stock and furniture on to upper floors where possible. An hour or so later they were being taken by RNLI crewmen in inflatables to the Phoenix Causeway roundabout and from there by ambulance to an emergency centre set up in Lewes Town Hall.

The water continued to rise throughout the afternoon and by dusk it had poured down Timberyard Lane into South Street which was soon a fast-flowing river along which the RNLI men manhandled the inflatables in which they were ferrying residents and their pets to higher ground. The power was cut off to the houses but the street lights stayed on throughout the night. Residents who had elected to stay put, and many of them did, watched anxiously as the water continued to inch up the front of their houses. Some were lucky with the levels and the water did not come into their homes. Others were not so fortunate.

As fast as it had risen the flood water began to fall, dropping in South Street by a foot between 4am and 5am on Friday. The tarmac on the crest of the road appeared, then the east side gutter emptied between Timberyard Lane and the entrance to the Lewes Rowing Club. Tesco's waterproof doors had kept its interior dry and when its surrounds were clear of water it was able to re-open at 10am on Sunday so shoppers could refill near-empty shelves and freezers.

BANGS FROM BELOW

13 October 2000

When the flooded water cleared the pavement outside his home in Malling Street near Cliffe Corner on Friday morning Nigel Clement noticed a paving stone had collapsed. From beneath it there was the sound of the banging which he diagnosed as arcing electricity and notified Seeboard. The pavement was taped off by the police and the fault had to wait its turn. The bangs continued throughout the day and the next night. On Saturday a crew arrived, dug down, and revealed the arcing cables from which the lead insulation had melted away. The fault was repaired and the lights in this part of the Cliffe came on again.

CHURCH AND GRAVEYARD RESTORED

2000

The millennium was marked in Malling by tidying up the overgrown graveyard of the parish church.

This was done during the ministry of the parish's first African priest, Yemi Lapido, a canon of Jos Cathedral, Nigeria.

He was also responsible for returning the church to its original orientation with the altar at the east end and seats either side of a central aisle.

In September 2002 Canon Lapido conducted his last service at Malling. He has retired and now in charge is Bishop Brian King, the recently-retired Bishop of Western Sydney, Australia, who is on an extended visit to this country.

A swan glides down a peaceful river, well within its banks again in the spring of 2003.

Settling in to a new century

2002

After the floods came the work of restoration and repair. It was 'business almost as usual' for some shops in Cliffe High Street within a matter of days – but a few still have not reopened. It was the same for householders. Some camped out upstairs until they could make their ground floor rooms habitable, while others were in alternative accommodation for a long time before builders approved by their insurers completed the necessary restoration work.

Various schemes for preventing future flooding have been put forward but so far no works have been undertaken on the east side of the Ouse.

Also still up in the air is the future of the Grey Pit at Southerham where it was proposed to have a park-and- ride car park. It is now being used as a dump for hundreds of discarded fridges and freezers.

Malling parish church at Christmas 2000.

*'To get rid of the load of irritation which my daily avocations occasion
I walked over Cliffe Hill and returned by Malling Hill. There
was a solemn grandeur and solemnity about the scene
which soothed my soul to peace and in some measure
tranquillised my emotions.'*

DR GIDEON MANTELL writing in his *Journal* on 15 June 1831

BIBLIOGRAPHY

Brent, Colin *Georgian Lewes,* Colin Brent Books 1993

Bennett, Elizabeth *My Memories of Lewes Over Many Years,* The Book Guild 1997

Cairns, B *Lewes in Old Picture Postcards,* European Library, Zaltbommel/Netherlands 1988

Connell, J M *Lewes. Its Religious History,* W E Baxter, Lewes and London 1931

Curwen, E C ed *The Journal of Gideon Mantell*, Oxford University Press 1940

Dunvan, Paul *History of Lewes and Brighthelmston,* 1795

Hill, A F *Port of Lewes in the 20th Century*, Unpublished paper March 2000.

Horsfield, T W *History and Antiquities of Lewes,* J Baxter, Lewes 1824

Kitch M J ed *Studies in Sussex Church History*, Leopards Head Press in association with
    Centre for Continuing Education, University of Sussex.

Lapido, Sue *A History of Saint Michael the Archangel*, South Malling Parish Church June 2002

North, James E *A History of the Jireh Chapel, Lewes,* Huntingtonian Press, Windmill Hill

Poole, Helen *Lewes Past,* Phillimore and Co. Chichester 2000

Ritchie, D *Quakers in Lewes,* Lewes Quakers 1984

Saltzman L F ed *The Town Book of Lewes 1542-1701*, Sussex Record Society

Smith, Verena ed *The Town Books of Lewes 1702-1837* and *1837-1901*, Sussex Record Society

Wadey, Bruce *The History of South Street Juvenile Bonfire Society 1913-1988*

Woollgar, Thomas *Spicilegia sive Collectanea ad Historian et Antiguatatis Municipii*
    Vicinioe Lewensis, 1812-1820, Unpublished MS at Barbican House, Lewes

Quarter Sessions Book 1642-1649 and *Custumals of Sussex Manors of the Archbishop of Canterbury*
Vols 54 and 57, Sussex Record Society, Barbican House, Lewes

Sussex Archaeological Collections. Sussex Archaeological Society, Barbican House, Lewes

Directories

Lewes, Newhaven 1881-2 W Tomkins 31 Sloane Street, Brighton

Lewes, Seaford, Newhaven and District 1951-1952 Silver Eagle Publications

Pigot and Co's Directory of Kent, Surrey, Sussex 1839

Bailey's British Directory 1784

Holman's Lewes Directory 1883

Kelly's Directory of Lewes 1964

Pike's Blue Book 1900-1980

Newspapers

East Sussex News

Evening Argus

Sussex Express and County Herald

Sussex Daily News

Sussex Weekly Advertiser and Lewes Journal

Magazines

Gentlemen's Magazine

Lewes News

Sussex County Magazine

Sussex Life

INDEX

Figures in bold refer to illustrations

INDEX

146

INDEX